Phoeb...
Refe...

SO, YOU THINK YOU'RE CLEVER?

Taking on the
Oxford and Cambridge
Interview Questions

SO, YOU THINK YOU'RE CLEVER?

John Farndon

ICON

This edition published in the UK and USA in 2015 by
Icon Books Ltd, Omnibus Business Centre,
39–41 North Road, London N7 9DP
email: info@iconbooks.com
www.iconbooks.com

First published in the UK and USA in hardback in 2014
by Icon Books Ltd.

Sold in the UK, Europe and Asia
by Faber & Faber Ltd, Bloomsbury House,
74–77 Great Russell Street,
London WC1B 3DA or their agents

Distributed in the UK, Europe and Asia
by TBS Ltd, TBS Distribution Centre, Colchester Road,
Frating Green, Colchester CO7 7DW

Distributed in Australia and New Zealand
by Allen & Unwin Pty Ltd,
PO Box 8500, 83 Alexander Street,
Crows Nest, NSW 2065

Distributed in South Africa by Jonathan Ball,
Office B4, The District, 41 Sir Lowry Road,
Woodstock 7925

Distributed in Canada by Publishers Group Canada,
76 Stafford Street, Unit 300
Toronto, Ontario M6J 2S1

Distributed to the trade in the USA
by Publishers Group West
1700 4th St.
Berkeley, CA, 94710

ISBN: 978-184831-932-5

Typeset in Plantin Light by Marie Doherty

Printed and bound in the UK by
Clays Ltd, St Ives plc

ABOUT THE AUTHOR

John Farndon, a graduate of Jesus College, Cambridge, is the author of numerous bestsellers on science, ideas and the natural environment, as well as being a playwright, composer and poet. His *Do You Think You're Clever?* (Icon, 2009) was shortlisted for the Society of Authors Education Award and he has been shortlisted a record five times for the Royal Society Junior Science Book Prize. He is currently writing *The Omnipaedia* for Square Peg.

Contents

CONTENTS

Introduction

So, You Think You're Clever?

A couple of years ago, I wrote a book entitled *Do You Think You're Clever?*. The question in the title is one of the legendarily difficult questions candidates for Cambridge and Oxford Universities sometimes get asked at their interviews. That first book was a selection of possible responses to this and an assortment of other equally tricksy questions that have actually been asked at interviews, such as 'Is nature natural?', 'What happens when you drop an ant?' and 'Does a girl scout have a political agenda?'.

Some people think these Oxbridge questions are just weird and pretentious. Or that they're designed as traps to frighten off any young students foolhardy enough to apply to those privileged pinnacles of learning – like some cabbalistic riddles or a trial of fire for budding Harry Potters. Of course, there probably are some dastardly tutors who do use them in this way – and I must admit that this how I saw them at first. But the brilliant thing about them is: they make you THINK. Aggravating and provocative as they are, they set your mind racing. That's what to my mind makes them fascinating for everyone, not just those applying to Oxbridge.

The thing is, most of us love thinking. We love

having our intellectual curiosity piqued, and it's the element of surprise in these questions that sparks the mind. The publishers of *Do You Think You're Clever?* and I were quite astonished by how well it was received, and how well it sold right across the world, from Korea to Canada. But I realised that the key to its success was that delight in thinking we all have. That's why I decided to have a go at another set of questions.

I'm sure a lot of people disagreed with my answers in the first book. I'm sure some thought they were rubbish. In fact, I know myself that I was guilty of a foolish error in a question about a man falling down a hole in the world, much to my embarrassment! But that's the point. Neither *Do You Think You're Clever?* nor this new book are meant to be about answers; they're about asking questions, and getting people thinking – and even flaws can do that (that's my excuse, anyway!).

There's no doubt, though, that some of these questions are seriously fiendish – which is why we came up with a Bond-villain variation on our original title, *So, You Think You're Clever?* You may imagine poor students moving slowly towards a revolving saw as they desperately try to come up with an answer – which may be what it feels like sometimes in an interview.

But another title we considered for this new book was *Do You STILL Think You're Clever?* This is an interesting and very Oxbridge-like variation on the awkward question in the title of the first book, of course, but it is in some ways even more awkward to answer. It's what's called a 'loaded question' in that it is based on an unjustified presumption that makes it hard to respond to directly without falling into a trap. Students of logic would call it a 'complex fallacy question'; I'd just call it plain mean. The first (possibly) unjustified presumption is that you at least once thought you were clever. From that flows the implication that if you answer 'yes' you're a fool if you haven't realised by now in face of all the glaring evidence to the contrary that you're not so clever as you thought; and if you answer 'no' you've seen how utterly mistaken you were in ever thinking you were clever. Either way you lose.

An apocryphal example of such a loaded question is to a witness in court who is asked, 'Have you stopped beating your wife?' The witness is incriminated whether he answers 'yes' or 'no'. In a law court, such questions might be described as entrapment, and the judge will usually steer interrogators away from them, but it's a technique journalists famously try.* And, of course, we

---

* Back in 1996, US Ambassador to the UN Madeleine Albright was apparently trapped like this when interviewer Lesley Stahl asked on the *60 Minutes* programme about the effect of UN sanctions on Iraq: 'We have heard that a half million children have died. I mean, that is more children than died in Hiroshima. And, you know, is the price worth it?' Albright replied 'I think that is a very hard choice, but the price, we think, the price is worth it.' – and immediately regretted it.

face such loaded questions every day, as when a girl asks her boyfriend, 'Do I look slimmer in this dress?' or a dad asks his truculent teenager, 'When are you going to grow up?' Fortunately, the consequences of failing to negotiate the traps set by some of the questions in this book aren't quite so perilous.

The responses I've suggested to these questions are by no means intended as definitive or even model answers. Far from it. I'm sure some interviewers would shake their heads in disappointment and turn me down flat. My intention is different. What I have tried to do is carry on where the question leads off – and provide you the reader with food for thought. Quite often, for instance, this means giving background information rather than responding to the question. Or it might mean going off on a flight of fancy. But what I've tried to do, throughout, is avoid technical jargon, or assume academic knowledge beyond that which most intelligent readers will normally have. My feeling was that interest in these questions shouldn't be restricted to subject specialists. After all, questions about the purpose of laws, or how to deal with world poverty, or what makes poetry matter, or just what makes matter – can be fascinating for us all.

Responding to these tricky questions is about being clever. But that's something that all of us can be. It's not about knowledge. It's not even about education. It's about bending and twisting your thoughts in all kinds of intriguing ways. And that's something *every-one* can do. It's certainly not the exclusive territory of those lucky enough to gain or even try for a place at Oxbridge. There's no bigger obstacle to genuine clever-ness than smugness.

And just in case you don't believe me, when I say everyone can do it, let me introduce the ultimate birdbrain.

A couple of years ago, a group of Cambridge sci-entists put some rooks to a test, to see if there was any truth in the famous fable by Aesop about the raven and the water pitcher. They put a nice, juicy worm float-ing on water in a long narrow tube, too narrow for the rooks to reach in and grab. So how would you get that worm if you were a rook?

The rooks were ingenious. They found stones and dropped them into the water one by one to gradually raise the water level until they could reach the worm. Damned clever, eh? Think about it. It means they not only had to know that putting stones in the water would raise the water level, but actually think of doing so and put it properly into practice. Almost creepy!

And if rooks can be so clever with their tiny brains, do you think all of us with our big brains could too? You bet we could.

Of course this book may help students applying for Oxford and Cambridge. But it is not just for them. It's for everyone, everywhere in the world, from Australia to Anatolia. We face difficult questions in the world every day – about where we are going, what we are doing – and we badly need new answers, new ways of thinking, thinking 'outside the box', and I hope these questions will help do just a little to make people think afresh, to think, yes, we could do this or that differently, we could try this instead. We don't have to make the same mistakes again …

How would you poison someone without the police finding out? *(Medicine, Cambridge)*

Clearly this kind of knowledge is essential for any Cambridge undergraduate. After all, you never know when your room-mate is going to become completely intolerable, or your tutor will fail you for what was without doubt the most brilliantly off-the-wall and original essay of the year. But why stop short at poison when there are all kinds of other ways you can do away with your academic cohort without detection? There are plenty of deep spots on the river for boating accidents, the old stone stairs in Grimm's Court are treacherous when wet, the chemistry lab is well known to be hazardous and Professor Dulles Ditchwater has bored at least a hundred students to death this year alone with his lectures, without any hint of a police investigation ...

But maybe I'm jumping to conclusions too fast. The question doesn't actually specify that my poison victim needs to die. A mild stomach upset might be enough to satisfy the questioner's rather disturbing interest in chemical suffering. I've certainly known one or two dinner parties where I've been most definitely poisoned by dreadful food or excesses of alcohol – and the police certainly didn't find out. In fact, a sure-fire way to poison someone without being taken by the long arm of the law is to take care the damage done by your poison is not severe enough for that blue limb ever to be extended in your direction.

So bad food and dodgy drinks at a dinner party are one way to trick people into swallowing poisonous substances without much likelihood of a crime scene investigation. But actually, many, many things can be poisonous in the wrong doses. As the 16th-century physician Paracelsus said, 'All substances are poisons; there is none which is not.' It's all about dose. In small quantities, vitamin A and vitamin D are essential for good health. But too much of either can be lethal. Even oxygen, the life-giving gas, can in excess harm the body. Of course, everyday drugs like paracetamol are lethal, too, in anything but the smallest doses, not to mention alcohol. And just by getting into a car and starting up you are poisoning someone, somewhere, since your car emits poisonous gases such as nitrous oxide, and soot particles which cause many people to suffer from lung disease. So the choice of poisons is vast.

This question is, I guess, though, about deliberately killing someone with poison. The attraction of poison as a murder weapon is its stealth and the fact that it requires neither strength nor much skill to administer. The assassin doesn't even need to be at the crime scene when the victim dies, which does make it much easier to get away with murder. That's why poisoners have always been looked at through history as a more sneaky and sinister brand of killer than honest-to-goodness sword slayers, straight-as-a-die gunslingers and no-nonsense axe murderers, though if you're the victim you're equally dead, whatever the method of your despatch.

History is littered with rulers and their rivals brought down by poison. Ivan the Terrible is said to have poisoned his wife and mother with mercury, and ended up a victim of mercury poisoning himself. The Borgias seemed to make poisoning a lifestyle (or deathstyle) choice, administering each other arsenic so frequently it's amazing the family lasted so long. Apparently, secretly adding small quantities of arsenic to a wet nurse's food was a neat way to kill an unwanted baby as the arsenic became concentrated in the nurse's breast milk. Who was the murderer?*

Poisoning was much more popular in the past than it is now, especially among the ruling class. That's partly because it was fairly easy to send a servant out to a backstreet apothecary and get a bottle of arsenic, no questions asked. It was also much harder to be certain a victim had been really been poisoned. Hamlet needed a ghost to testify that his dad was done in this way.

---

* One of the most appealing female poisoners, though, was Giulia Tofana, who lived in Rome in the 17th century. Giulia prepared poisons for young women trapped in difficult marriages to despatch their husbands with. She was such a heroine among these women that when the authorities finally found out about her trade and began to close in, they managed to keep her hidden for some time.

Nowadays, pharmacists are mostly averse to offering supplies of anything remotely poisonous, either over the counter or under, since nearly all potential poisons must be accounted for under Controlled Drugs laws. And your Google search for 'lethal poisons suppliers' will inevitably leave an incriminating trace on the internet or your mobile phone records.

Autopsies, too, can now pick up traces of most poisons in the body of a victim. So it's much, much harder than it was in the past to poison someone and get away with it, especially since we do now have proper police investigations. Forensic diagnostic tests are now so effective that it would be very, very difficult to poison someone without being found out, if the death was sudden and for any reason suspicious. Indeed, there are so few effective but untraceable poisons,* and those few so hard to obtain, that it really would be difficult to poison someone without the police at least finding that the victim had been poisoned. However, I have a much better chance of poisoning someone without the police finding out that it was me who did it.

First of all, it depends on the choice of victim. The more closely you are associated with your victim, the harder it is to avoid the finger of suspicion. So provided the questioner doesn't care who I murder (how

---

* I'm reliably informed that there are some sleeping pills which can be lethal in sufficient doses, yet are virtually undetectable in autopsies. But I'm not going to tell you what they are, even if I find out.

callous!), I've got a much better chance of getting away with it if the victim is a complete stranger than if it was my housemate or family. I could maybe knock off a few random strangers by dropping a grain of ricin* in the sugar bowl of a restaurant in another part of town, for instance. I'm unlikely ever to be suspected, especially if I cycled there and left minimal trace of my visit.

It might be straightforward, too, to poison drinking water supplies.† Mercury is relatively easy to obtain, and it is said by some people that al-Qaeda planned to poison water supplies in Iraq with mercury. And there are countless other toxic substances which if added to drinking water in sufficient quantity would make people very ill, even if it didn't kill them.‡ Indeed, many people have been poisoned by contaminated water supplies, at least negligently, if not deliberately.

I realise that I have so far not come up with any kind

---

* I say ricin, because it's absolutely lethal even in the tiniest doses, and it is possible to make it at home from castor oil seeds.

† One of the most horrific examples of this occurred in 1904, as a UN investigation finally revealed 80 years later. This was the German attempt to eradicate the African Herero and Nama peoples by poisoning the wells that supplied their drinking water. Many thousands died.

‡ In Britain's worst mass poisoning episode, thousands of people in Camelford in Cornwall in 1988 were supplied with drinking water contaminated by 3,000 times the permitted concentration of aluminium sulphate. Many people became ill and some are believed to have suffered grave long-term health problems as a result.

of methodology for poisoning someone I know – or even much detail on killing complete strangers. This is no bad thing. Even as an intellectual exercise it is an unpleasant line to pursue. A doctor needs to be aware of the effects and signs of poisons on a patient so that one might administer the right treatment. A forensic pathologist perhaps needs to know how poisons might be administered and how they might be hidden in order to track down a murderer. But otherwise, I think the idea of how to commit the 'perfect murder' is perhaps best left to crime novelists.

But maybe I could invite my victims to Japan, lay on a special treat of fugu pufferfish sashimi for them in a private apartment as a farewell gift as I head back home – then spike the chef's drink just before he starts to slice the fish. Fugu liver, of course, contains a lethal toxin, created when the fish ingests the vibrio bacterium, and if the sashimi is not cut perfectly, this toxin can lethally contaminate the food. It takes eight hours for the victims to die, and for a long time all they feel is a mild tingling before the fatal paralysis sets in. By the time the fish has done its dirty work, and the Japanese police have arrested the chef for criminal negligence, or manslaughter, I'll be safely out of the picture. And if the meal isn't quite as fatal as I hoped, I can always send ricin pudding as a birthday present by post from an old friend's neighbourhood.

Will this bag ever be empty? *(Natural Sciences, Cambridge)*

Never has an interview question sounded more like Lady Macbeth wracked with guilt over the murder of Duncan – 'What, will these hands ne'er be clean?' And so: the interviewer desperately shaking out an empty bag – the bag in which he carried away the corpse of the candidate whose answer was just a little too clever …

So to be on the safe side, let's start with a more mundane answer. This bag will be empty once I've removed all the visible contents. This is the everyday definition of 'empty'. So it can be emptied very quickly. All I need to do is turn it upside down and tip out my mobile phone, my lunchbox, my notepad and pen, my 'I Love Justin Bieber' T-shirt, my copy of *50 Great Ways to be a Genius*, and the envelope stuffed with fivers in case the interview goes badly …

But of course this empty bag is not really empty at all. Besides the dust, the crumbs, the fragments of scrap paper and millions of micro-organisms, it's actually still full of air, occupying every tiniest bit of space in the bag. As quickly as I remove every solid item, air rushes into the void. The movement of air molecules is so energetic and rapid that every space is filled instantly.

But what if I could remove the air? Would it then be empty? Perhaps I could suck the air out with a vacuum cleaner, in the same way as those vacuum bags that are sometimes used to store duvets. That would make the bag emptier. Of course, it would have to be rigid enough to withstand the air pressure outside without collapsing entirely flat – and absolutely airtight, which is highly unlikely. Even then, though, the best vacuum cleaner in the world can only create a partial vacuum. Physicists typically assess how near perfect a vacuum is by its air pressure. The lower the air pressure, the nearer it is to perfect. Vacuum cleaners get air pressure down by barely a fifth.

Much, much better vacuums are now achievable in ultra-high vacuum chambers in science laboratories and research institutes. So maybe I could put the bag inside one of these? That's certainly getting emptier. Yet even these scientific vacuum chambers are not perfect. They can achieve pressures as little as a trillionth of atmospheric pressure, but that's still not a perfect vacuum.

Okay, now I'm getting desperate. What if I put the bag on the next space flight to Mars and have it jettisoned into empty space, then leave it long enough for all its gas content to diffuse away into the void. That seems to be getting there. But even empty space is misnamed. In the emptiest of empty space there are a few hydrogen atoms in every cubic metre. So there are almost certain to be one or two lingering around in the bag and outside. There seems to be no way of physically getting it emptier than that. So I'm defeated.

Indeed, even if I were somehow able to devise a

way to capture and remove those last elusive hydrogen atoms, I'd suddenly discover the futility of the exercise.

The concept of emptiness has long been a conundrum for thinkers of all kinds. On a very simple level, there is a problem with definition. If there is nothing between us, then there is nothing between us – so we must be adjoining. It is semantically impossible for emptiness to occupy any space at all.

Classical thinkers such as Aristotle argued that nature contains no vacuums because denser material would always rush in instantly to fill any void. Aristotle is said to have coined the phrase 'Nature abhors a vacuum'. Indeed, he went further and said that a void is conceptually impossible, since there is no such thing as nothing. He believed therefore that empty space between matter is filled with an invisible medium. Democritus, on the other hand, insisted that the world is just atoms in empty space, writing in his typically acerbic fashion, 'Nothing exists but atoms and empty space; all the rest is opinion.'

This debate about what occupies the space between matter was still raging 2,000 years later, as Newton argued that the space between worlds must be filled with an invisible, frictionless medium to provide a framework for the normal laws of motion to operate in, while Leibniz insisted that the solid bodies of the universe alone were enough of a framework and that all else was empty space.

Meanwhile, Galileo and Torricelli were showing

experimentally that vacuums could really exist. They upturned a closed glass tube filled with water (later mercury) – and saw a void open up in the top of the tube as the water dropped away. Since no air could get into the tube, this void must be a vacuum. Further experiments showed that this vacuum could be changed by, for instance, seeing the void grow when the tube was up a mountain where air pressure was lower. If a vacuum can be affected by physical changes it must have a physical reality.

Over the next few centuries, scientists experimented and achieved better and better physical vacuums – yet no one really knew just what a vacuum is. The idea of some invisible medium between atoms persisted in the concept of the 'ether' – the mysterious medium many scientists felt was needed to carry waves of light and electromagnetic fields. Then in a groundbreaking experiment in 1887 Michelson and Morley showed there was no ether that had any kind of measurable existence. So it seemed that maybe my empty bag really could be empty.

And then came quantum science. Quantum science has turned the notion of emptiness completely on its head. Quantum science shows that a particle such as an electron is only probably in one place. Indeed, all particles and fields are just fluctuating probabilities. If my bag was perfectly sealed from the universe outside and contained nothing but a perfect vacuum, there will still be an electric field inside the box surging this way and that, positive and negative, with quarks bubbling up all over the place in response. The overall electrical energy might average out to zero, but this vacuum energy* is still measurable.

So my perfectly empty bag is actually a seething ferment of quantum energy, with waves and particles popping in and out of existence. The energy fluctuates continually, and when it is at its lowest possible level it is said to be in a vacuum state, but even in a vacuum state there is some energy.

Indeed, some theories suggest our universe is simply a fluctuation of vacuum energy. Like particles in a quantum vacuum, our universe popped out of nothing. Shakespeare's King Lear was proved wrong when he said to his daughter Cordelia, 'Nothing will come of nothing.' So it may be with the universe. Something did come out of nothing. The trouble is, it is a fluctuation, so might just as well vanish back to nothing again, like a bursting bubble. This bag may well be empty sometime, and so might the universe – until another one pops into existence. And who knows, bags might have become empty and universes might have vanished millions or billions of times before.

----

* In fact, it's now believed that empty space is filled with vacuum energy that's creating the pressure that's driving the universe apart against the pull of gravity. In recent years, distant supernovae suggest the expansion of the universe is not slowing down but accelerating, and it is this dark vacuum energy that may be responsible.

How would you market a rock band?

(Economics and Management, Oxford)

The days when a band could just hone their music, play a few gigs and wait for word to spread are largely gone. Nowadays, if a band is not to simply fade away, ignored and forgotten, behind the bedroom door, it pretty much has to become a marketing organisation, too. Indeed, for some bands, marketing actually comes before the music – quite literally. A band I know launched a successful marketing campaign and raised enough money from fans through crowdfunding to pay for studio time – all before they'd ever played a note together!

There's no doubt we live in a world where marketing is king. When the Industrial Revolution rolled into the world two centuries ago, business was about products. 'Build it right,' industrialists sagely advised, 'and they will come.' But by the 1930s, there was so much product that businesses had to go out and sell! sell! sell! to beat the competition. Today, with choice and information making consumers more discriminating, the stress is more and more on marketing.

Indeed, many businesses nowadays are actually little more than exercises in marketing, geared wholly to identifying what customers want and when they want it, and trying to meet those needs. And it's not just the marketing staff engaged in marketing, but everyone from creatives to production staff. Even writers like myself are pulled into the marketing frenzy. What most publishers want from us, essentially, are not great books but great hooks. And that's so for rock bands, too.

So my very first task when marketing a rock band would be to identify the band's 'hook', their USP (unique selling point) – that distinctive and special quality that's going to tell the fans this is who they want to listen to, hang out with and buy the music of. Until I've got that hook shaped up, I can't begin to market them properly.

I'm going to talk about marketing a new totally unknown and unsigned band, using only my own and the band's meagre resources for a marketing campaign, not a mega budget from a big record label.

The band I want to market is an all-girl metal band that call themselves the Cleaners, because they got together when bassist Su and vocalist Imo met working at night, cleaning offices, to bring in the cash – something they still do. Their music is sombre but there's a real sly sense of humour. So, assuming they agree, I'm going to get them to change their name to the Night Shift Zombies, and describe them as the (rock) spirits who come out at night to clean up the crap of the human day.

I don't want to play up the zombie side too much, since that's been done to death, as it were, but the idea is to make cleaners, and other low-paid young night workers (of which there are millions), just a little bit cool. I'm going to help the band appeal to those who feel marginalised, exploited, futureless, driven to the dark places – and of course night shift workers. It's a niche market, but a very big one, and tightly focused. The Night Shift Zombies' music is already coming from this place, so all I'm doing is targeting their market rather than turning them into something they're not.

Brand-building will be key, assuming the music is good (though that's not vital). So before I start on the outreach side of marketing, I need to 'develop the product'. I'll need, for instance, to get the band develop their look and dress sense – subtly, not overly theatrical to keep a sense of authenticity – with just hints of the zombie cleaners. I'm going to get a stylist friend of mine to select items from their wardrobe to give them a glam but slightly nightmarish cleaner look – and I'll get some very moody, cool-looking shots of them in an office late at night surrounded by cleaning products and a pile of sad rubbish left by all-too-dull daytime office workers. I'll need them, too, to showcase and develop the songs which connect most with the target audience. Rock bands' appeal is tribal, so I want a tribe of alienated night shift workers to identify with them, and make them aspirational. Humour and a tongue-in-cheek approach will be important. 'Yes, we know night cleaning is a rubbish job and not a mission, but we're all really cool people ...'

What I hope I've done here is identify what some

marketers now call a *solution* – that is, I've spotted a need in the market and tailored a product to suit it. The three other elements I'll then need to develop, according to some market theorists, are *information* (telling people about it), *value* (the value it has for users), and *access* (letting people access the band's music where and when they want to), creating the acronym SIVA – solution, information, value, access.*

For a rock band, making money is a long-term goal. So value is less of an issue. The aim has to be to first create a following for the band, then monetise it later. So it's information and access that are the priority elements in marketing after the solution. A great deal of this is going to come via the internet, of course, as I'll come back to. But it's a mistake to forget about traditional methods altogether. Tangible products like

---

* Marketing theorists have been rather hung up on such abbreviations ever since 1960, when E. Jerome McCarthy introduced the four Ps – product, price, place and promotion. In 1990, Robert Lauterborn updated the four Ps with the four Cs – consumer, cost, communication, convenience. Lauterborn argued that customers didn't only consider price of a product, but the total cost, such as the cost of accessing it, the cost to their image of buying an uncool product, and the cost to their conscience of buying something harmful to the planet. They also resented being manipulated by pushy promotion and marketing worked best if it communicated with the customer, establishing a dialogue. Now many marketers talk about SIVA, which emphasises a softer, more interactive kind of marketing more appropriate to today's internet-savvy, more sceptical consumers.

T-shirts, badges, stickers and so on, do have an impact, because they linger in a way that briefly read internet mentions don't. A cool girl or guy walking around wearing a striking T-shirt with the band's name and logo on can bring the band's name to attention quite effectively, for instance.

But of course the internet is where I'll need to put the bulk of my marketing efforts, because of its huge power to reach the target market. Setting up an attractive website for the band, plus a Facebook page and a Twitter account are crucial first steps. Then I want to step up access to the band's music by sharing certain tracks on sites like Bandcamp and Soundcloud. The more people that listen to the Night Shift Zombies, the better. Sites like NoiseTrade could work really well. You give users of the site free access to tracks, but in return you get their email addresses – and emails addresses are gold dust for marketing, enabling personalised marketing that even social media can't manage. In the early stages of a band's career, it's going to be emails that matter more than social media. I'll need to recruit a dozen or so keen supporters to act as starting points to continually generate internet traffic among their friends and their friends' friends to get the ball rolling. The social media and email traffic about the band needs to be continuous and escalating. That's why I'll lean on the band members and their supporters to put effort into blogging and tweeting.

What's also important is to identify and target the media and internet outlets that are likely to have a specific interest in the NSZ, rather than wasting time with blanket marketing. I will approach the bloggers, interest sites, radio stations and so on that take a particular interest in their brand of music – and try to establish as a good a personal relationship with each one of them as possible, so that they listen to the band, play their music, follow what's happening and so on. Marketing today is about personalised relationships with the customer – or interested parties.

Live gigs are going to be important, because these are crucial in establishing the dedicated fan base that moves things forward – and also provide news items to keep people interested. So I will try to get the band gigging in as many venues where regulars are likely to appreciate their music as possible.

And of course YouTube videos are probably the single most valuable marketing tool. They needn't be expensive, but they've got to be really distinctive to make an impact among the many thousands of band videos uploaded each day. I want to make the video an event. I'm going to find a suitable office space we can use out of hours – it can be abandoned rather than in use – and shoot the band playing a gig here in front of as big an audience as we can get of suitably attired night shift workers. The song we select will be one with a bit of humour, and we'll edit it to make the most of the humour, since this seems to be key in getting videos to go viral. We'll contact all the cleaning firms and other businesses doing similar night shift work, and also put an ad in the 'cleaners wanted' section of outlets like Gumtree, inviting them all to come along and participate in the making of the video. We'll also send out a press release to all the media outlets, telling them about this event.

After that, we'll be on a roll. O2 Arena here we come. With luck, in half a century, people will look back on the 2010s as the era of the Night Shift Zombies just as they do on the 1960s for the Rolling Stones ...

Is Wittgenstein always right? *(French and Philosophy, Oxford)*

If you say so, and I say so, then we both agree, and no more needs be said. Wittgenstein's argument was that there is no such thing as truth in an ultimate, reducible sense, and that Western philosophers have got waylaid searching for it, hunting it down like scientists at CERN chasing down the 'God particle', the Higgs Boson, with their atom smasher. It's all about language games and shared meanings – well, not all, but partly, as I'll make clearer.

I must admit I was quite surprised when I first learned a little more about Wittgenstein's ideas. His ideas seemed so lost in obscurity and high-flown thought that I was surprised to find he even lived in the 20th century. I'd somehow got a picture of him wandering around medieval Germany in a cowl muttering dark and impenetrable remarks that made fools of everyone around, a kind of alchemist of the intellectual. I guess I was going a little Shakespeare then, conflating Hamlet and Wittenberg and Guildenstern.

Yet although I'd got my dates fabulously wrong (he lived from 1889 to 1951), the image wasn't entirely off the beam. There was something rather Garbo-esque in the glamour Wittgenstein gave to philosophy, and in the apparent moodiness with which he withdrew from the academic life after writing his first book – as if you half-expect him to mutter 'I vont to be alone!'. When Wittgenstein was in the room, apparently, even the most brilliant speakers somehow felt their words were rather superfluous, and maybe they secretly wished he would keep himself to himself a little more.

Wittgenstein's point about truth emerged in his first book, translated into English in 1922 as *Tractatus Logico-Philosophicus*, the only book published in his life. It's quite a short book and notoriously opaque. But it seems to have managed a quite thorough demolition job on the whole of Western philosophy, which is perhaps why Wittgenstein gave academic philosophy up after writing the book and turned to teaching in schools, presumably feeling there was no more to be said.

Philosophers, Wittgenstein said, had made the mistake of being like scientists chasing the meaning behind things – truth, mind, time, justice, reality – when none of this really matters, or is even achievable. A philosopher might waste his time wondering how he knew the child with the cut knee screaming her head off was really in pain, while the mother would rush in with comfort and bandages. The philosopher was clearly the one with lessons to learn.

The mistake, Wittgenstein argued, is in thinking philosophy can answer these questions. It comes partly from a flawed view of language that insists that if a word has meaning, there must be a thing attached to that meaning. The philosopher asks, 'What is reality?',

'What is justice?' or 'What is the mind?' and then goes looking with logic for the identity of that thing – and of course can't find it, because they are just words. That's why the search has gone on fruitlessly for centuries. But if you remember that language is variable, and words simply mean what people understand them to mean in a particular setting, the problem vanishes. That's why if you say Wittgenstein is 'right' and I understand what is meant by 'right' in this context, no more needs be said.

Indeed, Wittgenstein challenged the idea of logic as an ultimate arbiter of truth. $2 + 2 = 4$ is not an ultimate truth, he asserted, but just something that makes sense arithmetically. If you were to say $2 + 2 = 97$ it would not be false – just nonsense. The philosopher's task is to reveal such nonsenses.

Deciding whether a proposition is logically true or false is entirely missing the point, Wittgenstein went on to say, since language has many other meaningful uses. This may seem a trivial observation, he admitted, but that's the point. Philosophy 'does not teach us new facts, only science does that,' he wrote. 'But the proper synopsis of these trivialities is enormously difficult, and has immense importance. Philosophy is in fact the synopsis of trivialities.'

In later, unpublished works, Wittgenstein talked about 'language games'. People play with language and use it differently in different contexts. They learn an assemblage of changing meanings by association. What matters is the way a word is used, not its meaning. A bad ball means two very different things to a cricketer and a society butterfly. Neither leads to an ultimate truth; they are simply different usages.

Wittgenstein talked about the famous duck–rabbit illusion, first published in the German magazine *Fliegende Blätter* in 1892. This looks like a drawing of a rabbit – until you suddenly see that it is also a duck – and vice versa. Neither is right or wrong; they are simply different ways of seeing.

In some ways, Wittgenstein was suggesting that poetry and music and art have more to teach us about the meaning of life than science and philosophy, and that their contribution was underrated. Indeed, for him, philosophy was a poetic pursuit rather than a scientific one. So just as there can be no poem that is 'right', nor can there be any philosophy which is right – but that's not to say that either cannot have great power and meaning.

Wittgenstein's reputation has fluctuated since his death in 1951. At first, there was quite a widespread rejection of his ideas – understandably, perhaps, since his ideas seemed to jettison the ideas of some of the greatest thinkers of the Western world, while at the same time expressing himself so obscurely that many couldn't understand them entirely, or couldn't be bothered to wade through them. More recently, though, there has been renewed interest in his ideas.

'To be or not to be; that is the question,' posed Hamlet. Perhaps Wittgenstein would have said it depends on the way people understand it. Interestingly, Tom Stoppard wrote an ingenious comedy entitled *Dogg's Hamlet, Cahoot's Macbeth* based on the ideas of Wittgenstein, in which a group of children are rehearsing *Hamlet* but understand it so little that it may as well be a foreign language. In fact, the children speak in a language called Dogg, which is made up of English words but with entirely different meanings assigned to them than the usual ones. In the play, in a scene based on Wittgenstein's posthumously published *Philosophical Investigations*, a builder calls his assistant for such items as 'slab', 'pillar' and 'beam' and the assistant delivers them as if he knows what items these words mean – but he may simply know already what to deliver, and simply understands these words as cues. The words could just as well be 'one' 'two' and 'three'. So if you ask 'Is Wittgenstein always right?' I might answer, 'No, he is sometimes all that is left.'

How small can you make a computer?
(Engineering, Cambridge)

This is a question that's been much in the minds of computer engineers recently, and the short answer is: very, very small indeed. Already by 2013, we had a fully working computer no bigger than a grain of sand. It's designed to be inserted right into the eye to monitor glaucoma, which is why, with a nice touch of wit, it's called the Micro 'Mote' after the biblical speck in the eye.* It's got processing, data storage and even wireless communication, and is solar powered by light coming into the eye.

And the EU's Pico-Inside project has made a simple logic gate that's quite dramatically smaller than this. It has the logic power of fourteen transistors yet is made from just 30 atoms. That means it's not only too small to be seen under any optical microscope; it's too small to be seen by anything but the most powerful scanning tunnelling or atomic force microscopes. So you could fit about a quintillion of these little processors inside the Mote!

Back in the late 1960s, computer pioneer and Intel founder Gordon Moore noted something remarkable. In 1958 two transistors had been linked together in an

---

* 'And why beholdest thou the mote that is in thy brother's eye, but considerest not the beam that is in thine own eye?' (Matthew 7:3)

integrated circuit inside a silicon crystal to create the first 'silicon chip'. Ever since, Moore observed, the number of transistors that could be fitted inside a chip had doubled every year. Since then, electronic devices have gone on shrinking by the year in accordance with 'Moore's Law'.

The pace of miniaturisation has slowed down recently and the number of transistors doubles only every two years. Still, it has given us all the amazing 'smart' devices we have at our disposal today – tablet computers, phones with the computing power of a supercomputer of not so long ago, and so on. Every time someone suggests that miniaturisation has reached its limits, computer technologists seem to succeed in squeezing electronics into even smaller spaces.

So the question is, how much further can the shrink go? One might also ask, why would you want anything smaller?

It seems we are indeed coming close to just as far as we can go with conventional transistors. They are already down to the nanoscale – billionths of a metre (the size of viruses). But there may be problems with going much further. Transistors work as 'gates' turning on and off the flow of electrons. They are made of 'semiconducting' material that can be switched on and off to conduct electrons or block them off. But once the barrier gets down to about a nanometre (nm), quantum effects come into play. In particular, quantum tunnelling occurs. Quantum tunnelling is when an electron tunnels right through the barrier as if wasn't there. (Actually it doesn't 'tunnel' through at all, but simply disappears one side and reappears the other side.) If the gate can't be shut to electrons because of quantum tunnelling, the transistor cannot work. The smallest transistors now are just over 30nm across, so this limit may soon be reached.

Transistors provide the logic gates on which computing depends: the yes/nos, and/ors, 0/1s. If transistors reach their limit, could logic gates be created in another way that circumvents this quantum limit? That's what the Pico-Inside team and others are working on. Instead of trying to squeeze more and more computing power into an ever smaller space, they are starting from the bottom up, seeing if they can build a computer bit by bit from atoms, so that they can take advantage of quantum effects rather than being defeated by them. To move the atoms around to build such computers, they work with atomic force microscopes to nudge the atoms into place. So far, besides the 30-atom logic gate, they have assembled atoms to make vehicles, gears, wheels and even motors, each consisting of a single molecule. It's long way before they create anything that remotely resembles a working computer, but the possibilities are clearly there.

One problem with these nanocomputers is not the processing power but all the peripherals. How can they be powered? How can they be kept cool? How can they communicate with other devices? It's no good building a computer the size of a molecule if it then needs a wireless add-on a trillion times as big to send its data, or a solar cell or battery even bigger. And of course solar cells won't work in dark places. So these are problems that need to be solved if nanocomputing is ever to become a reality.

Something even more dramatic than the nano-computer could be achieved by abandoning the simple logic gate of the transistorised computer altogether with 'quantum computing'. The aim here isn't to make a small computer, but to harness the power of quantum effects to achieve hugely faster speeds, which might end up meaning the same thing. And to make a quantum computer you have to scale things down anyway to the level where quantum effects come into play – that is, the level of atoms, electrons and even photons. Quantum computers, if they are ever built, will harness atomic or subatomic particles to be processing units.

The idea is that instead of the bits in a conventional computer, which are just 0 or 1, you use quantum bits or qubits, in which bits are superimposed by quantum effects to be not just 0 or 1 but can also be both at the same time. With conventional computers, the bits have to run through all possibilities sequentially when making a calculation. With qubits, they can all be tried simultaneously. That means a computer could solve a problem many millions of times faster than a conventional computer by working on problems in parallel.

In 2014, Canadian company D-Wave hit the front page of *Time* magazine with what they claimed was the first commercial quantum computer. The D-Wave is the size of a large wardrobe and works – but no one is sure yet whether it is actually a quantum computer. Neither are they yet sure what the benefits of such a computer might be. So far, it's been suggested that it might help banks steal a march in financial dealings by making super-fast calculations, which would give it real commercial value, but its overall value to mankind is not yet so clear.

This is one of the issues with tiny computers: what's the purpose? Why would you want a computer the size of a grain of sand, when it's easy enough losing your super-slim mobile around the house? There are at least two answers to this.

The first is that devices the same size as your mobile could have dramatically increased computing power so they can do all kinds of fantastic things they can't do at the moment. Critics say, though, that this is the wrong way to go about things. There is no need to increase the power of individual computers. Instead, you increase connectivity, so that the computing power of all computers linked into a network is used simultaneously, as in cloud computing. That way, the power of your individual terminal can be quite small, because it taps into the power of the cloud.

The second is that nanocomputers could be deployed to enable us to manipulate things on a nanoscale. The most exciting possibilities are inside the body. I've already talked about the Mote operating inside the eye. Nanocomputers could be inserted into the bloodstream to monitor blood flow, or help make other diagnoses with on-the-spot reports. One tiny computer might not do much, but swarms of nanocomputers swallowed in a simple pill might help break down cholesterol in the blood, or perform a swift inside job to remove kidney stones.

Other scientists talk about harnessing the power of organic molecules, to make biodegradable computers that can work inside living cells, maybe deactivating cancer cells, or delivering drugs to particular cells.

The vision of our bodies being continually repaired from the inside by swarms of unimaginably tiny computerised devices is certainly a beguiling one, if somewhat unnerving. It could be, if realised, the most astonishing breakthrough in medical care ever. And nanocomputers could be used in many other fields, from cleaning pipes from the inside to building drugs molecule by molecule.

All this is some way off, and the problems with building, powering and connecting with such devices are considerable. But 60 years ago who would have imagined computers could ever be so small and powerful that they could do things we now take for granted, such as connect to the internet from a tiny phone, pretty much anywhere in the world?

Personally, I couldn't make a computer any smaller or more complex than an abacus right now, but there are people who can. But I've thought of an even better way: I could participate in the making the finest computer known – a human brain. Even when fully grown, the human brain is amazingly small for its power – the most powerful ever known. How do you fancy making a supercomputer tonight, darling?

How do you organise a successful revolution? (History, Oxford)

If a lot of media commentators and academics are to be believed, modern revolutions, from the Arab Spring to Euromaidan in Ukraine, are driven by social media. If they are right, then being a revolutionary is a rather comfortable calling. I don't have to dress up in dark combat clothing, cover myself with anarchistic badges and tattoos, write dense and frightening theses or even learn how to build a bomb. All I have to do to get my revolution going is sit at home in my pyjamas with my laptop, open a twitter account and get tweeting, #vivelarevolution!*

---

* Social media have certainly been in the spotlight in these recent upheavals. The protests in Iran in 2009 have been dubbed the Facebook Revolution. The Tunisian revolt in 2011 was dubbed the Wikileaks Revolution. The Egyptian revolution of 2011 was called the Twitter Revolution. And Ukraine's Euromaidan has earned the same soubriquet.

The social media provided news of what was going on that was beyond the control of conventional media. They told personal stories that drew people in. They allowed the sharing of ideas and opinions. They made the coordination of protests such as those in Cairo's Tahrir Square much easier. According to some sources Facebook usage in Egypt went up 2 million in the first three months of 2011 as the protests got under way, and Facebook usage doubled across the Arab world at this time.

But the question asks how to organise a 'successful' revolution, and at once the limitations of the idea of Twitter and Facebook as engines of revolution become more apparent. For a start, it's clear

First of all, though, I've must decide the aim of my revolution. It could be just a small, everyday kind of revolution – the kind that advertisers mean when they trumpet the revolutionary cleaning power in their new detergent. But why not think big? Let's go for the overthrow of global capitalism and its replacement with small-scale people's socialism around the world. I want to see the power and money taken out of the hands of the nexus of global corporations, financial networks and shadowy NGOs and shared between communities of people at a local level. So how do I go about it?

When the Russian socialists wanted to overthrow

---

that the success of all these so-called social media revolutions varies widely and is hard to assess. Only Tunisia seems to have moved smoothly to a new liberal constitution and democratic government, while Egypt remains in transition. The conflict in Syria is no nearer resolution for all the use of social media – and right now the future of Ukraine's Euromaidan is in jeopardy because of a threat that is very real and non-virtual, the Russian army.

Interestingly, as a social media event, the Egyptian revolution of 2011 was a success. Social media allowed many well outside the direct tow of events to feel deeply involved. Millions of people around the world followed the occupation of Tahrir Square on social media, feeling a sense of engagement and solidarity far beyond simply listening to the news. But it was like a TV drama that played itself out towards an apparently successful denouement after just eighteen days when Hosni Mubarak left office and the occupation ended. The considerably more messy reality of ensuing events, much less followed on social media, is harder to rate as a success, with the military back in power and Egypt's first elected president Mohammed Morsi still on trial.

the power of the Tsar and foment a Marxist revolution, they became bitterly divided over two possible approaches to revolution. There was the Menshevik line, which ultimately was a slow-burning long route, building grassroots support and bringing people gradually on board. The Bolshevik approach, advocated by Lenin in his famous paper of 1901, *What is to be done?*, was much more urgent and called for a small, determined vanguard of revolutionaries to take over the levers of power right away and drag the people with them.*

I have a lot of sympathy with the Bolshevik idea. After all, the problems created by global capitalism are indeed pressing. People need change now, today. Even one more child dying from hunger, one more life blighted by poverty, is one too many. But the historical precedents for this approach are none too happy. It was men (mostly) far too thoroughly convinced of

---

* The Mensheviks, who led the field in the 1917 Russian Revolution, believed revolution had to begin with the liberal bourgeoisie and democratic capitalism, but they were soon swept away by the Bolsheviks, led by Lenin and his vanguard. And when Lenin died in 1924, the theoretical argument, at least, came down to a battle between the ideas of Stalin, who pushed for 'socialism in one country' – the brutal industrialisation of Russia to bring it to the level of the Western capitalist countries – and Trotsky, who argued that the only way to sustain the revolution was 'permanent revolution' – spreading the revolution across the world until there could be no turning back. But of course, Stalin's triumph and Trotsky's demise were only little to do with theories.

the rightness of their cause to brook any opposition that brought the Terror of the French Revolution, the indescribably appalling purges of Stalin's Russia and dreadful suffering in Mao's China.

Indeed, countless revolutions driven forward on this basis have ended in bloodshed and pain – and this is perhaps inevitable because who is to say who should hold the levers of power? The Irish political philosopher Edmund Burke predicted long ago, at a time when English radicals and romantics were still thrilled by the first triumphs of the French Revolution, that the overthrow of the status quo would lead to infighting between factions and a power vacuum that would be filled by a military dictatorship – a prediction that has proved itself again and again, not just with Napoleon but with Stalin, and many others.

I might be able to organise an effective revolution with the top-down approach, but I don't think it could ever be a successful, lasting revolution.* Success

---

* For a long time in the historical past, a revolution could not be, by definition, a success. A revolution was a disaster, a collapse in the normal order of things, a descent into chaos that was to be avoided at all costs – the world turned upside down. That doesn't mean revolutions didn't happen, or didn't ever change things for the better. There are countless examples of what we now call revolutions throughout the ancient world, as rulers such as Julius Caesar overreached themselves and got their comeuppance. But the downfall was generally seen even by supporters as a grim necessity, not the welcoming doorway to a bright future.

depends, I believe, on a bottom-up approach that has the overwhelming support of the mass of people. The sheer size of the task of getting large numbers of people on board puts many would-be revolutionaries off this idea, especially when it seems the status quo pulls all the strings. It's tempting to believe, in your desperation for change, that the only way to effect a revolution is to get to pull the strings too, only in a different direction.

But the key, I think, is to remember that I don't need to bring the revolution by myself. All I need to do is share my ideas. If enough people come to believe the same thing, then change will come, and come powerfully and unstoppably. As one person in a world of 6 billion, it might seem as if I am isolated and powerless to effect change. But if my vision is a good one, it can spread quickly among huge numbers of people.

It was only from the mid-17th century that revolutions began to be seen by many as a vital step in the progress of mankind towards a more enlightened, fairer world, as moribund or tyrannical regimes were consigned to the past. And Karl Marx, of course, argued that revolution was an ultimately inevitable stage in the progress of mankind. Scholars have spent countless words analysing what triggered the revolutions of the 17th to 20th centuries, and in particular the English 'Glorious Revolution' of 1688, the American Revolution of 1765–83, the French Revolution of 1789, the Russian Revolution of 1917 and the Chinese Revolution of 1927–49, and though the interpretations are hugely varied, all seem to agree that these revolutions only occurred because the time was ripe. In other words, there were enough people, or enough people of the right kind (whatever that might be), were receptive to, or even desperate, for change.

Back in the 1960s, American psychologist Stanley Milgram became famous for the idea of 'six degrees of separation' – the theory that, because we are all linked by chains of acquaintance, we are each just six introductions away from any other person on the planet. In other words, all I need to do is so thoroughly persuade a few people that I meet of the rightness of my ideas that they are equally willing to try and persuade others that they know. In this way, my idea could spread around the world person-to-person with astonishing speed, helped, of course, by electronic social media. My problem is, at the moment, that my idea is not yet persuasive enough.

With the person-to-person campaign under way, I'd also try other routes of persuasion. As a writer, of course, I see the attraction of the media, so I'd look for avenues to get my ideas across through various media, from books and TV to YouTube, Twitter and other social media. But I know this won't be easy, since the control of the media agenda on a larger scale is very much in the hands of the powers I'm trying to reduce. So I have to try other avenues to bring my ideas to wider attention.

One tried and tested route is to initiate newsworthy events. Peaceful occupation of key city squares seems to be one way to go. The occupation of Tahrir Square in Cairo and Maidan in Kiev by just a few thousand people got both of them worldwide attention that prompted change, because they were so much in the news that they were hard to ignore – especially since they were accompanied by avid social media attention. Whether either of these examples will be successful revolutions still hangs worryingly in the balance – and of course in many places such occupations would be dangerous or impossible, such as Syria. But with the aid of social media, an action like this is certainly an achievable goal.

As yet, though, the aims of my revolution to overthrow global capitalism are too vague to resonate with people, and such a protest, in the comparatively comfortable 'developed' countries of the world, is more likely to meet with quiet bafflement among the majority than mass support – as the Occupy movement discovered.

So first of all I have to spread my ideas and convince enough people it is time for change. And if I get impatient, maybe I could hire a hypnotist to address key meetings such as the G20 summit, the Bilderberg summit and the UN and use the power of suggestion to persuade the assembled politicians and plutocrats that they would be much happier personally if they were to become the heroes of the gentle revolution that banished the evils of global capitalism from the world for good. Actually, perhaps, I should just try to persuade them of that anyway, with long personal letters to each ...

If there were three beautiful, naked women standing in front of you, which one would you pick? And does this have any relevance to economics?

(PPE, Oxford)

What an absurd, offensively sexist question! I'm going to assume the questioner is being deliberately provocative to make a point. The idea of posing such a question is indeed deeply relevant to economics, or rather to economists, and in particular to a misguided strand of economic thinking that presents human choices in terms of hypothetical games.

Choice has been at the heart of much economic theory ever since Adam Smith wrote his great book *The Wealth of Nations* in 1776. Choice is the very essence of the logic of the free market. If left free, Smith insisted, the market will always expand to produce the right amount of goods because it is guided by the invisible hand of self-interest, expressed through our choices.

If people are left to make free choices, the theory goes, it will produce the best results for the economy and society, and maximise people's welfare and well-being. Twentieth-century theorists like Milton Friedman and Friedrich Hayek argued that no one can know better than you what's in your best interest – and any attempt to guide your choices, such as state allocation of resources, is doomed to failure. A free market, they suggested, lets you do far more than choose what to buy; it allows you to choose how you live your life.

In an attempt to pin down the effects of choice mathematically, economists in the post-war years in the USA in particular developed the idea of rational choice theory. The underlying assumption in this theory is that we are all 'individual utility maximisers'. That means each of us is focused entirely on getting what's best for us. In other words, every choice we make in life is a rational pursuit of our own self-interest and inner desires (you can begin to see where the question comes in).

It's a very neat way of looking at how choices in the marketplace can be analysed and predicted mathematically, which is why it has come to underpin a vast swathe of economic thinking in the last half-century, and has spawned a number of influential theories.

One of these was Kenneth Arrow's social choice theory. Arrow used the 18th-century political thinker Marquis de Condorcet's three-way voting paradox* to show that consensus is impossible (the 'impossibility theorem'). So all political decisions – however well-intentioned – must be an imposition on individual liberty, Arrow stated, and only the market mechanism

---

* Condorcet explained that in a three-way electoral race, the outcome can easily be deadlock – and then, whoever wins, two-thirds of the electorate will have preferred someone else.

can make valid social choices.* (Again there are echoes of our question, with its three choices.)

Another theory to emerge from rational choice theory is game theory.† Game theory tries to mathematically pin down the choices people make as if they are games of strategy between two players who are each trying to win at all costs. It's rational choice theory in its most abstract, purely mathematical form, and has been applied to everything from how people shop to animal evolution. Its classic example is the 'prisoner's dilemma' game in which two accomplices in crime are imprisoned separately – and promised a shorter sentence if they spill the beans on their accomplice. According to the theory, the only rational choice is for each to assume the worst of their accomplice and squeal.

---

* 'In a capitalist democracy there are essentially two methods by which social choices can be made: voting, typically used to make "political" decisions, and the market mechanism, typically used to make "economic" decisions' – Kenneth Arrow in *Social Choice and Individual Values* (1951).

† Game theory was the brainchild of John von Neumann, the extraordinary and brilliant Hungarian emigré later pinpointed by many as the model for the unhinged nuclear scientist Dr Strangelove in Kubrick's film. Von Neumann invented the theory in 1928 but it first hit the headlines in 1946 following the publication of the book he wrote with Oskar Morgenstern entitled *Theory of Games and Economic Behaviour*, written while simultaneously working on the Manhattan Project to develop the atom bomb.

The big problem is that scientific experiments that try to replicate games like the prisoner's dilemma with real people show that people actually very rarely behave like this. Most people have an innate sense of fairness and trust, and do not base their choices on calculated self-interest alone. Indeed, games like the one suggested by the question – which woman do I pick and how will she respond? – have only a tangential relationship to real-life behaviour, thank goodness.

Rational choice and game theory paint us in a very odd and rather contradictory way – as calculating, highly logical robots driven only by our individual animal desires. But actually we are very complex beings, and this is only part of the picture. On the one hand, we very rarely behave with complete rationality. On the other, we are social animals whose need to relate well and connect to other human beings often far outweighs our desire for self-gratification. That's why consensus, for instance, is not only possible but, ironically, desirable.

Amazingly, though, a whole edifice of economic theory and policies has been built on rational choice theories and dreadful laddish choice games like the one posed by the question, even though they bear little resemblance to how people really behave. Theories like this underpinned the charge to liberalise and deregulate markets in the 1980s and 90s, and shaped the economic models that guided policies which ended so disastrously in the global meltdown of 2008. Since then, great champions of rational choice, such as Alan Greenspan, the retired head of the US Federal Reserve, have admitted that economists got it badly wrong – and in recent years 'behavioural' economists have begun to challenge the orthodoxy of rational choice.

The problem is that many economists still believe that posing and trying to answer questions like the choice between three naked women actually illustrates something about the choices we make in real life. With a massive leap from reality, some might talk about its relationship to Akerlof's 'market for lemons' theory (originally devised in relation to buying dud used cars), which was about the choices people make when they're uncertain of just what they're getting – a dilemma which the removal of the women's clothes seems to avoid. The conclusion would be that you would go for the most beautiful of the three. Others might talk in terms of 'hedonic pricing' or of 'an experience good' – a commodity that you only have full information about once you've experienced it.

The whole idea of speculating like this is, of course, deeply unpleasant, and only something an (usually male) economist would find instructive. For a start, my own response to this bizarre hypothetical situation is hugely more complex and nuanced than any orthodox economic analysis would allow. Secondly, it completely ignores the massively offensive idea of my being able to 'pick' one of these women like some slaves at a market

– and the utter stupidity of not considering they might have any mind or influence in the matter.

I am going to hope the interviewer was indeed hoping to provoke me into challenging orthodox economics and the absurdity of the 'dilemma'. If not, and the scenario was posed in all seriousness, I may just have cost myself a place – and earned myself the ridicule of the three women standing completely astonished as I rambled on about economic theories and missed out on all the fun ...

Do you believe that statues can move, and how might this belief be justified?

(French and Spanish, Oxford)

Yes, statues can indeed move. How about the Venus de Milo, the exquisite statue carved by the Ancient Greek sculptor Alexandros in Antioch in what is now Turkey some 2,100 years ago? Venus now sits in the Louvre in Paris, far from where she was found on the island of Milos in 1820. During the Second World War, she even went on retreat to Valençay in central France to escape the conflict. And who knows if she didn't journey from Antioch to Milos of her own accord, since there is no evidence to prove that she didn't.

Then there's the French quarter-scale replica of the Statue of Liberty. Mini-Liberty was originally set on the Île aux Cygnes in the Seine in 1889 facing the Eiffel Tower to the east. But in 1937, at the time of the Paris Exposition, she was turned west to face her original as she does today.

So of course, statues can move by human agency. They can move entirely naturally, too, as they are provoked into motion, perhaps, by earthquakes or volcanoes, landslides or floods, tempests or tornadoes, or elephant stampedes, or even a bad attack of wood-worm in floorboards. Indeed, no statue is ever still, since it is forever swept around at high speed as the Earth rotates on its axis and orbits the sun. Of course, since all motion is relative, you could say the statue is motionless relative to the ground. But then no statue could ever be said to be completely still while the atoms that make it up are in motion, as they will be until the sun stops shining and temperatures drop to absolute zero. Indeed, the miracle would be to find a statue that cannot move.

So statues can certainly move physically. And of course the finest statues can move emotionally, too. The powerful spiritual and sexual charge of Bernini's famous Ecstasy of St Theresa moves many people who go to see it in Rome. And the French master Auguste Rodin's great statue of the Burghers of Calais moved local councillors to fury when Rodin tried to insist it should have no pedestal – and no doubt Rodin was equally moved to fury when the councillors mounted it on a pedestal despite his wishes.

At the heart of this question, probably, though, is the strange and ancient fascination for reports of miraculous statues that apparently move entirely of their own accord. There are many fictional stories of statues that come to life, of course. The best known is Ovid's story of the sculptor Pygmalion who carves a statue of a girl so beautiful he falls in love with her. Pygmalion then goes to the temple of Aphrodite and prays earnestly to the goddess for a girl like his statue, which he calls Galatea – and when he returns home the statue has come miraculously to life, ready for him to marry. And

then there is the wood carver Geppetto and his delin-
quent boy puppet Pinocchio.

Yet there are countless reports throughout history,
too, of 'genuine' miracles of moving statues. It seems
there is a recurrent wish for these to happen as visible
evidence of the divine, or of mysterious forces in the
world. Maybe it's because statues seem to dwell so close
to the border between inanimate object and the miracle
of life, appearing human yet completely lifeless.

Just how much people want to believe in these
phenomena was shown by the excited reaction to a
video posted online by Manchester Museum in the
summer of 2013. The video was a time-lapse sequence
showing a small Ancient Egyptian statue of the deity
Neb-Senu rotating mysteriously on a shelf. The video
rapidly went viral, and online chats were soon buzzing
with a frenzy of theories to explain Neb-Senu's little
turn. The suggestions ranged from the mundane and
practical to possession by the god or an ancient curse.
So there was a sense of disappointment later in the
year when a team of investigators revealed a more
down-to-earth explanation – that a slight prominence
on the base of the statue allowed it to swivel as it
was vibrated by the movement of traffic outside the
museum. But the museum had never had so much
attention.

Actually, it wouldn't have surprised the Ancient
Egyptians at all to see a statue of a god moving

miraculously. In fact, they expected it. Apparently, when Ancient Egyptians went to receive an oracle from a god, the priests often animated the god's statue to add extra weight to their words. It's unclear if those consulting the oracle knew the statue was being moved by the priests or if they really believed it was moving miraculously. I suspect that they mostly knew but accepted this as part of the ritual, and since the priests were holy, the difference between the hand of god and the hand of a priest was not so great anyway. They willingly accepted the deception.

The Ancient Greeks, too, liked the idea of animated gods. Daedalus, father of the Icarus who had an unfortunate flying accident, made statues that walked, so the story goes, and were so lively that they had to be tied up at night to stop them walking off!* The legendary smith Hephaestus was also said to have made fantastic metallic moving statues known as automatons – most

---

* Daedalus's statues were apparently so famous that Plato invoked them to make a point in his dialogues:

Sokrates: You have not observed with attention the images of Daidalos. But perhaps there are none in your country.
Meno: What is the point of your remark?
Sokrates: That if they are not fastened up they play truant and run away; but, if fastened, they stay where they are ... To possess one of his works which is let loose does not count for much in value; it will not stay with you any more than a runaway slave: but when fastened up it is worth a great deal, for his productions are very fine things.

famously Talos, the mechanical giant said to have guarded Crete.

These stories are generally dismissed as fictions, but the Greeks were capable of building highly sophisticated mechanical devices, as the Antikythera Mechanism bears witness. The Greek poet Pindar describes how you could often encounter moving statues in the streets of Rhodes:

> The animated figures stand
> Adorning every public street
> And seem to breathe in stone, or
> Move their marble feet.

In 13th-century Turkey, the Muslim polymath Al-Jazari became famous for his fantastic humanoid automata, and subsequently many other mechanical maestros built ingenious automata, including Jacques de Vaucanson with his Flute Player of 1737. In the late 19th century, French workshops churned out thousands of beautiful clockwork automata which are highly sought after by collectors today. Nowadays, with modern electronics and motors, animatronics can create spectacularly convincing moving statues.

But the target of the question, perhaps, is not these mechanical and electronic marvels, but the apparently miraculous motions of religious statues reported by devotees throughout history. Such reports are especially common in Catholic countries such as Spain, France and Ireland. The statues rarely get up and walk in these stories – rather, they roll their eyes, or move their lips, or cry, or drip blood.

Statues seem to be particularly lively in times of trouble and worry. The sceptical might say people are highly susceptible to such delusions at these times, when they are seeking the comfort of a sign from God, or quite often Mary the Holy Mother. Believers might say that Mary is offering the comforting reassurance of miracles at a time of need.

In Ireland, in 1985, when the country was wracked with doubt about changes to the abortion laws, reports of moving statues came thick and fast, culminating in the report by two teenage girls of the movement of a statue of Mary in a grotto near Ballinspittle in July, and children's reports of black blood flowing from a statue of Mary in Mitchelstown.

What's interesting is that in most of these cases, witnesses only ever said the statues *appeared* to move, rather than claiming the statues actually moved physically. It is therefore hard for objective observers to prove or disprove their story. Some psychologists explained them as optical illusions, or the effect of mass hysteria. But the witnesses, of course, believed that what they were reporting was genuinely a divine message meant especially for them. If other people could not see the apparition, it was simply because the message was not intended for them. No further justification was necessary for those who received the message.

This creates a conundrum. If I don't witness the appearance of movement myself, and can't employ any scientific methods to test for it, then I cannot say it certainly occurred, but neither can I say with certainty that it didn't. And merely because, for instance, I cannot capture on camera or any other scanning device, a movement that a witness sees, I cannot justifiably say the witness is deluded. It's supposed to be a miracle – and if the miracle means the witness sees the movement but the camera doesn't, that could simply be part of the miracle. All I can say is that it contradicts all the normal ways of testing the veracity of events.

I certainly don't think all those witnesses are lying – that is, knowingly telling untruths; nor do I believe all, or even most, are mentally prone to delusions. They are, mostly, sane people who are telling their story truthfully. My personal belief is that the movement is, though, entirely a creation of the witness's brain and that there is no physical reality to their reports. But it is much harder to dismiss the mental reality as nonsense. It is real for the witnesses, and it would be foolish to insist that my more material view of reality is the only viable one. My hearing is less than perfect, so I miss many sounds that other people hear. You'd rightly tell me I was a fool if I said that because I can't hear them, they don't exist.

Why do human beings have two eyes?

(Biological sciences, Oxford)

Romantics might say that a pair of brown eyes is just for loving, but I guess we need a more scientific answer here.*

It's not only humans that have two eyes, of course. So too do all vertebrates: mammals, amphibians, reptiles, birds and fish. So doubling up of eyes is deep-rooted in evolution. In a way, then, we humans have two eyes because our ancestors far back on the evolutionary tree did – and we've kept them because no mutation since has proved better. Two eyes seem to be an unbeatable adaptation for us vertebrates as a way to see the world. In fact, many features of the body double up, with the left half of the body almost a mirror image of the right, with only a few major organs such as the heart and liver being single. So one might say we have two eyes for the same reason we have two ears and two knees.

Yet there is also something about human eyes that's

---

* Actually, this is not so off the point as it might seem. Forward-looking eyes play a key part in fostering the relationships that make us human, and maybe so successful as a species. Because our gaze is so directed, it's quite clear who we're paying attention to, and that helps form bonds. It's why we're pretty much alone in making love face-to-face. And it helps us form bonds not just with other people but animals that have the same forward-looking eyes, like dogs and cats – and it may be why we find baby animals, whose eyes face forward more than those of adults, so cute.

rather different from the eyes of most other two-eyed animals, and rather special. Nearly all other vertebrates, from fish to fieldmice, have eyes either side of their heads, looking sideways and moving independently, which gives them pretty much all-round vision at all times. With us humans, both our eyes face forward, and move together, which reduces them, effectively, to a single eye. Only other primates, and a handful of predatory animals such as owls and hawks, wolves, snakes and sharks have similar frontal vision. For us to have given up the advantages of multi-directional two-eyed vision, we must get some major advantages from this single-direction frontal vision, and it turns out that we do.

For herbivores and other prey animals, all-round vision is a huge advantage because it allows you to see danger coming from any direction. Even while you've got one eye on the grass you're eating, your other eye can swivel to catch a glimpse of a predator sneaking in from behind.

But many predators don't need that panoramic scanning at all. What they need is to home in on their target. Primates don't need all-round vision, either, because up in the trees there is a limited number of directions predators can attack from. What they need is to be able to precisely judge distance as they swing through the branches, or try to grab fruit. A single misjudged jump might easily wipe your genes from the evolutionary tree.

The evidence is that the different predators and the primates both evolved frontal vision separately but they both developed forward-facing eyes because frontal vision confers on them an advantage that both need – that is, judgement of distance. Two eyes facing forward give us humans, and those other animals, what is called binocular vision. The view through both eyes is nearly identical but, because they are a little way apart, not quite identical – that slight difference is crucial.

Most of the time, we hardly appreciate that there is any difference, because we just see a single picture. But hold two fingers up, one in front of the other. Then focus on the nearer finger and shut first one eye then the other. You'll see the further finger shift its position dramatically. Similarly if you turn your fingers sideways and focus your eyes on a distant tree, you'll see that your two fingers become four.

What is remarkable is that your brain combines these two slightly different views, technically known as a disparity, to give a single view with an impression of depth. It's called Leonardo's paradox because the great Renaissance genius was baffled by how two eyes with different views could ever give a single picture. Yet he also realised that this single view with depth allowed us to see a world in three dimensions, a world of solid objects, not flat pictures, and despaired of ever painting pictures that could do justice to it.

What Leonardo didn't realise was that it was the

unification of that very difference in view in the brain that gives us 'stereo' vision, the impression of depth. That key insight was provided by a simple experiment performed in 1838 by English physicist Charles Wheatstone, who took drawings of the slightly different views seen by each eye through a device he had invented called a mirror stereoscope. The stereoscope allowed him to present the views separately to each eye – then together to each eye. When he presented the views together, he found the pictures suddenly leaped into wonderful 3D.

Key experiments by neuroscientist David Hubel and Torsten Wiesel in the 1960s showed that the image created on the retina of each eye registers in exactly the same place in the brain – overlaying each other precisely to create the unified, single view we see whenever we open our eyes. Then Australians Jack Pettigrew, Horace Barlow, Colin Blakemore and Peter Bishop discovered that the slight differences also register in the brain, and it is these slight differences that give the single picture its special 3D quality.

The 3D effect is greatest close up, because that's where the difference between the picture shown by the two eyes is greatest. It diminishes further away. Laboratory experiments suggest the 3D effect should work at up to 2.7km away, but tests in real life suggest it never goes much further than 200m.

Binocular vision is not the only way we judge

distances. Perspective, change of focus, and visual clues such as objects being partially hidden when they're behind something all help us build up our impression of a solid world. So someone with a single eye is by no means incapable of judging distance. Indeed, we are so accustomed to our 3D view of the world that we can shut one eye and still see in 3D. That's slightly harder, though, for someone who has only ever had vision in one eye.

What is remarkable, in some ways, is just how perfectly the eyes move together. For the unified view to work, the image on each retina must be identical, barring the slight differences in viewpoint, and they must change identically as you move your eyes. The retina is tiny, so even a tiny difference would destroy the unity. When the eyes move laterally, this is called version. Actually, these movements are happening automatically all the time, although we're not aware of them. Our eyes are constantly darting this way and that, always perfectly together, as we scan the scene before us. Saccades, as they are called, are the fastest movements in the body, shifting the eye through 900° to and fro every second at peak.

Besides these lateral movements, your eyes will stay focused on the same thing quite easily even when you move your head. What's more, they will move in opposite directions easily to focus on objects near or far. When they focus on an object nearby, they turn towards each other, in a movement called convergence; when they focus on something further away, they swivel away from each other a little, or diverge. When convergence is overdone, you become cross-eyed, of course, but that's rare.

Clearly the eye muscles must be perfectly coordinated to manage version and vergence with such accuracy and precision. But that wouldn't be nearly enough. In fact, the control doesn't come from the muscles at all; it comes directly from particular parts of the brain's frontal cortex, known as the eye fields, which track the pictures on the retina and feed back signals to the eye muscles to keep the eyes perfectly coordinated.

Now that we understand how binocular or stereo vision works, we have found a variety of ways of mimicking it by feeding slightly different images to each eye, just as Wheatstone did in his famous experiment. 3D films are now commonplace, shot on cameras that take two views, from two slightly separated viewpoints. But you need special glasses to view them, to allow each eye to see the two pictures separately, so they are far from perfect. And the disparity between the viewpoints must be carefully worked out with simple equations to give the right baseline (the distance between the two lenses), otherwise the picture will look very odd.

In some ways, our binocular vision is our key evolutionary advantage. Our forward-looking eyes, our precise judgement of distance, our ability to look and control what we're doing with our hands with such precision – whether we're threading a needle or throwing a spear at a fast-moving animal – all depend on this remarkable difference from most other animals. It's something other primates have, of course, but we humans have really made the most of it.

Was Shakespeare a rebel? (English, Oxford)

Shakespeare is the very pinnacle of English heritage, his plays a colourful pageant of kings and queens, lovers and buffoons, paraded in their pomp and historical glory in the finest English language. Shakespeare is The Bard, the Swan of Avon, the hallmark of English culture and pride, the poster playwright for all that's finest in the nation's traditions. He is a veritable gift for the tourist industry to rank alongside our royals and our museums, but also a vital prop for those conservatives who look to history for a sense of worth and stability. And generations of unwilling schoolchildren have been fed a diet of Shakespeare partly because ultra-traditional educationalists have insisted that it is as good for the children as Latin and deference.

This image of Shakespeare as not so much a pillar of the establishment as an entire suite of lavishly appointed chambers has had academic backing too. During the Second World War, at the same time as Churchill was delivering stirring speeches with cadences ringingly echoing Shakespeare, Cambridge don Eustace M.W. Tillyard wrote a hugely influential book of literary criticism entitled *The Elizabethan World Picture* (1942). In it, Tillyard argued that the Elizabethans and Shakespeare in particular inherited and amplified the medieval worldview of the Great Chain of Being in which everything and everyone has a rightful place, and which cannot be broken without disrupting the peace and harmony of the world. This view, some critics might say, presented Shakespeare as a propagandist for the monarchy, writing dramas that glorified Elizabeth I, the Virgin Queen, as the head of the body politic. Tillyard wrote a second landmark book, *Shakespeare's History Plays* in 1944. That same year, Laurence Olivier gave a celebrated film performance of one of these plays, *Henry V*. With Henry's St Crispin's Day speech, it stirringly brought to life the image of the heroic monarch leading the country, just when the war-ravaged country needed it.

Tillyard has often been criticised since, and numerous academics have pointed out that the Elizabethan World Picture was a Tudor myth, presented by Elizabeth to gain stability for her regime in turbulent times, when Protestant England was deeply threatened by the forces of Catholicism, and another invasion.* Many have gone on to say that Shakespeare's plays present a far more

---

* Elizabeth's rousing speech to the troops assembled at Tilbury to meet the expected invasion of the Spanish Armada in 1588 seems as if it could have stepped straight from a Shakespeare play: 'I know I have the body of a weak, feeble woman; but I have the heart and stomach of a king, and of a king of England too, and think foul scorn that Parma or Spain, or any prince of Europe, should dare to invade the borders of my realm; to which rather than any dishonour shall grow by me, I myself will take up arms, I myself will be your general, judge, and rewarder of every one of your virtues in the field.'

nuanced perspective than simply glorifying stability and continuity. But only a few have gone as far as to say he was a political rebel.

Yet, in some ways, it should be a surprise if he was not. Great artists think differently from other people – it's what drives them to create – and this makes it all too likely that their way of thinking will therefore run counter to the establishment. There have been few, if any, other great artists who have been true apologists for the status quo. After the great Russian poet Alexander Pushkin died in a duel, the young poet Lermontov lamented him as a victim of the imperial regime. But when the tsars fell, Pushkin was quickly appropriated by the tsars as one of them, representing the glory of Russian culture, and then by Soviet Russia, who presented him as one of them instead, a liberal rebel oppressed by the tsars. And so the view on his political allegiances has yo-yoed back and forth. In other words, we should be wary of seeing Shakespeare as he is commonly presented.

Shakespeare was living in one of the most turbulent times in English history. It was very far from the glorious and peaceful Garden of England presided over by a benign queen that still lingers as an image in films, stories and even history books. Henry VIII's dramatic split from Rome was still red raw. Elizabeth's Protestant regime was under attack from Catholics both from within and without, with the Spanish Armada beaten

off only with a certain amount of luck and Mary Queen
of Scots imprisoned and finally executed for fomenting
rebellion. Just as Elizabeth's elder sister Mary had ruthlessly tried to suppress protestant opponents, earning
her the sobriquet 'Bloody', so Elizabeth's henchmen
were relentless in sniffing out and punishing any signs
of Catholic recusancy. A network of spies organised by
Francis Walsingham hunted down Nonconformists and
those who would not sign the oath of allegiance, and
courts devised methods of execution of barely imagi-
nable cruelty for those caught.

For England's many Catholics, then, Elizabeth's
regime was a reign of terror, not so different from
that for dissidents living in Stalin's Russia. It was a
time when numerous houses had priestholes, secret
escape routes and hiding places for the paraphernalia
of Catholicism – and of course there were plots and
counterplots galore. People began to get used to talking in riddles, and poems especially were full of codes,
acrostics and double meanings which only those in
the know would understand. Nowadays such riddles
are presented as exuberant Elizabethan wordplay.
But that's surely a misreading; this was a matter of
life and a very nasty death for many people. Mary
Queen of Scots was condemned to death because of
an intercepted message in code. It's in this context that
Shakespeare was writing.

Of course, his plays are thoroughly steeped in

politics. The implications of kingship, law, governance, authority, obedience, abuse of power – and rightful and wrongful overthrow of rulers – run through play after play, from the history plays to *Macbeth*, *King Lear*, *Hamlet* and even *The Tempest*. Shakespeare does write about domestic issues and about romance, but even in plays such as *Romeo and Juliet* and *A Midsummer Night's Dream* there is a clear political streak. Indeed, how could it be otherwise in such politically charged times? A great writer would have to be half asleep not to let some of the issues of the day filter through into his work. And certainly others were deeply aware of the political power of Shakespeare's plays. *Richard II*, for instance – a play about the overthrow of a failed monarch – was given a special staging at the Globe on the very eve of the Essex rebellion against Elizabeth in 1601. The players were lucky to escape with a warning when the rebellion failed. The question is, what way did Shakespeare's politics fall? Was he carefully apolitical, was he pro the status quo – or was he indeed a closet dissenter or even a secret rebel?

The interesting thing is that while there is a flood of politics in Shakespeare's plays, there is an extraordinary absence of religion. It's their secular basis that has kept his work accessible and relevant today. Of course, very few dramatists of the day brought much religion into their work. Maybe they thought church and stage didn't mix – even though theatre had strong roots in religious drama. Or maybe they thought religion was just too hot a potato. And yet it is odd that Shakespeare, who tackles such big issues head-on, should apparently come nowhere near the burning (literally) issue of the day.

A few years ago, Clare Asquith wrote a controversial book entitled *Shadowplay*. As the wife of a diplomat in Soviet Russia, Asquith witnessed the subversive way Soviet playwrights played games with the censors with hidden messages that were all too plain to those who understood. She began to wonder if Shakespeare was working in the same way. In the book, she makes a detailed case for Shakespeare being a secret rebel, a Catholic recusant, who brilliantly laced his plays with hidden pro-Catholic messages and symbols – not quite overt enough for him to run the risk of imprisonment or worse, but clear enough for many in the audience. This way he didn't avoid the religious issues of the day at all, but tackled them in metaphor and code instead. If she's right, though, Shakespeare was playing a dangerous game.

Asquith suggests that the metaphors 'low' and 'dark' always mean the Protestant church, because they espoused low church values and often wore black, while 'high' and 'fair' mean Catholics. Many of his heroines are sunburned to show they are exposed to the sun, the symbol of God's truth, and so on. She suggests a startling alternative reading of the line in Sonnet 23 which always looks like bad grammar: 'More than that love which more hath more expressed.' She suggests it is a reference to Thomas More, Henry VIII's chancellor who was beheaded for refusing to deny the supremacy of the Pope. For those in the know, the line would read: 'More than that love which More hath more expressed' – that is, the ultimate love, the love of the martyr.

The jury of consensus is still very much out on this argument, but it is at least beguiling. The idea of Shakespeare playing cat and mouse with the censors is a thrilling one, and certainly spurs you to read the plays again and look for evidence oneself. Of course, that can be a dangerous game, leading you to find things simply because you're looking for them. But the emotional commitment Shakespeare gives to characters who show defiant integrity against the odds does hint at which side he was on. It's not clear that even if Asquith is right, though, that it necessarily makes Shakespeare a secret rebel. But it's a question worth asking.

Would Ovid's chat-up line work?

(Classics, Oxford)

The title of Ovid's 2,000-year-old poem *Ars Amatoria* is usually translated as 'The Art of Love', but that makes it sound rather too refined and heady. It'd be better translated as *The Lover's Guide*, or retitled *57 Steps to Seduction*, because it's far more down-to-earth, and reads more like an instructional manual than a highbrow discourse on romance. In fact, it's not so very different from the 'helpful' guides to getting a girl (or boy) you see online, complete with brief videos to show the techniques in action. Even the kind of instructions Ovid gives are not so different, right down to their essentially sexist premise. In the hands of a ruthless editor, and tarted up with some flip ironic straplines, some of Ovid's advice could even make it into the pages of *Loaded* or a downmarket girl's mag.

But that bit about the editor is crucial. Reduce the *Ars* to just the basic instructions and you've lost what makes Ovid's poem great. The *Ars Amatoria* has sustained interest for 2,000 years not because of the effectiveness of its advice but because it's written in sparkling Latin verse, with the wit, wordplay and rhythm that puts Ovid among the finest poets of all time. Even though the content is lowbrow, it seduces the ear of those familiar with Latin with its brilliant craftsmanship in the same way that Mozart can entrance with just a simple but uniquely perfect melody. In the face of Ovid's consummate poesy, its success as a guide to bedroom consummation becomes (almost) redundant. And of course the liberal lacings of classical references continually reveal Ovid's intelligence and erudition in a way that no modern instruction manual ever would.

Actually, the classical references hint at another purpose of Ovid's, which is not necessarily picked up by all readers. To me, the poem is quite clearly tongue-in-cheek. It's a send-up of both the great epic poems of the ancient world and of high-flown ideas of romance. Maybe his urbane readers are never going to experience the thrill of an Achilles wielding his mighty weapon in conflict outside Troy but they can become heroes instead in the battle of the sexes, and learn to be expert soldiers in the field of seduction.

Principio, quod amare velis, reperire labora,
Qui nova nunc primum miles in arma venis.

('First, the girl you desire to love, you must strive to
    encounter,
You who are taking up arms now as a soldier of love.')

And love is not something between gods and goddesses, but a game you play with the girl you met at the circus or in the marketplace.

The poem's attitude to women is, as you might expect, rather sexist, treating them as fair game to be tricked and seduced, and stressing the need for girls to dress up, shave their legs and prepare for their man. This is Ancient Rome after all. But it's less condescending than many contemporary lads' mags, and it's leavened with a wit and consideration for women that is often far more appealing. And remarkably, Ovid devotes the entirety of the third book to helping women turn the tables and learn the tricks they need to catch and keep their chosen man. In some ways, behind the banter and the braggadocio, Ovid seems to be making a genuine plea for mutual fulfilment in relationships.

That said, just how effective are Ovid's chat-up lines? Chat-up lines always get a bad press. Out of context, most sound so cheesy you'd be lucky if the girl or guy of your choice didn't expire from nausea on the spot.*

So you might guess that no chat-up lines really 'work', neither Ovid's nor anyone else's. The whole idea that a single line, or technique, is a sure-fire way to initiate any worthwhile relationship, seems absurd,

---

* For example:

'Are you an interior decorator? Because when I saw you, the entire room became beautiful.'

'Are you religious? Because you're the answer to all my prayers.'

'Did you hurt yourself when you fell from heaven?'

'Do you know the big difference between sex and conversation? [No.] Do you wanna go upstairs and talk?'

'Do you believe in love at first sight, or should I walk by again?'

and anyone trying them – or falling for them – seems rather desperate.

And yet there are (not entirely scientific) pieces of research occasionally reported in the tabloids, and even psychological journals, that suggest that they do work on some level. They may not, if you're a man, convince a girl that you're husband or long-term boyfriend material, but with some girls, even the ripe Stilton versions may at least convince them that you have a sense of humour (or not) or that you're confident (or not), both of which can be appealing in the short term. It all depends, of course, on the basic attraction, how you deliver the line, and how you follow up. Those same surveys suggest that a chat-up line, if it doesn't bring instant rejection, is simply the opening gambit in a longer process of mutual exploration that preludes any kind of relationship. And this is where Ovid comes in.

In fact, Ovid doesn't actually offer any glib chat-up lines at all. What he does offer are tips on dating, and his dating advice seems pretty sound even today, if somewhat obvious. (Their appeal is in the way he introduces them.)

If you want to get a girl, Ovid says, you can't just expect a girl to fall out of the sky; you have to put in the work and go out and look for one. He suggests good places to meet girls, such as the circus or theatre, and that's pretty much as any dating adviser would say now, though they might ditch the circus and throw in an art gallery opening or a small music gig. Of course, Ovid didn't have access to online dating sites.

Before you go to meet girls, or out on a date, Ovid says, make sure you're clean – you don't want to smell like a farmyard. Keep yourself well-groomed and fit – and trim that nose hair. All of this seems pretty sound advice too. He also advises you not to get too carried away by a girl or guy you see only by candlelight or when you're drunk. In fact, most of his suggestions seem fairly sound even today. You might be better to avoid his suggestion, though, of proving your keenness when faced by a shut door by climbing into the lady's house through the skylight or down the chimney. That way you're most likely to end up in jail or at least with a restraining order. Some things were clearly very different in Ancient Rome.

In summary, Ovid gives you no better or worse advice on dating than pretty much any good modern dating guide; it's the kind of advice that most people know anyway. But reading Ovid in Latin, if you can, is a whole lot more fun and elevating than reading a manual, I suspect. And saying you just read *Ars Amatoria* in the original Latin may be one of the most effective chat-up lines of all, with the right girl (and a complete turn-off for the wrong one). So maybe time to get conjugating …

Instead of politicians, why don't we let the managers of IKEA run the country?

(Social and Political Sciences, Cambridge)

Over the last 30 years or so, there has been an increasing move towards privatisation of government and public services in many Western democracies. In the UK, for instance, major nationalised industries, such as the railways, telecommunications and power were sold off by the government to private, profit-making businesses in the 1980s, and more recently the Post Office has been sold, while more and more elements of the National Health Service and education have been contracted out. So why indeed don't we take the logical next step and privatise the whole business of government?

I have a feeling that if you conducted a poll using this question, a large proportion would consider it a good idea. The choice of private institution in the question is clever. It doesn't ask why don't we let government be taken over by the managers of BP, or Lloyds Bank or Rio Tinto – vast corporations whose reputations have all come under fire. Instead, the question talks about IKEA, a company who deal directly with the public, and make what seems cheap, neatly designed furniture with an image of Scandinavian style and neatness.

IKEA's image seems clean, efficient and essentially benign rather than possibly rapacious or dirty. There is no connection at all between the running of a country and trim Scandinavian furniture, but the association creates the appealing idea of a country run along the same clean, efficient and benign lines. As influential American psychologist Edward Bernays showed in the 1930s, the power of association is huge. People might be much more hesitant to put power in the hands of a BP or Rio Tinto, even though their managers might be equally efficient.

The sleight of hand involved in this question is part of a pattern of media representation that has encouraged people to look favourably on privatisation – and distrust politicians as incompetent, out-of-touch and venal, and public administration as overbearing, obsessed with red tape and utterly inefficient.*

The argument might run that IKEA managers are experts in management – and that they are forced to be experts because they need to achieve bottom lines.

---

* Behind this lies, at least in part, the rise of rational choice economic theories, which have driven a wave of deregulation, privatisation and tax reduction to lift the so-called deadening hand of government, while the idea that politicians and public servants are not to be trusted, encapsulated in the related public choice theory, has become so ingrained in our cynical modern age that we assume it's true. There has been a massive shift away from the idea that people enter politics or the civil service to serve the public good. Interestingly, the description 'public servant' has all but disappeared, in favour of 'bureaucrats'; they are thought of as not only self-interested but as easily dispensable dead wood.

Politicians are not expert managers at all; they are simply good at talking and negotiating. So politicians (and public servants) are good at creating red tape, but if you want something actually done, go to the experts. Moreover, the IKEA managers will always be kept efficient by the profit incentive. If politicians get things wrong, they may not even get voted out if they contrive to pull the wool over the public's eyes.

But there are two huge problems with this argument. The first is the idea that the only way to get things run well is to give people a selfish incentive such as profit. It's led to the deeply flawed assumption that by definition private profit-making companies do things better than publicly run institutions. Proper evidence and research tends to disprove this assumption and show that nationalised industries can often be actually be more successful than private businesses – as the nationalisation that turned South Korea into one of the world's rising economic powerhouses shows. Indeed, many public institutions are very well run by administrators who are able to see the bigger picture and not become blinkered by a drive for profit.

The emphasis on incentives in private business has often led to a damaging short-termism. Most business theorists, for instance, espouse the idea of shareholder value maximisation (SVM) – the idea that managers are rewarded with bonuses and share options according to how much they give to shareholders each year. But because shareholders can simply move on if dividends are low, SVM has led managers to prioritise immediate profits in order to hang on to shareholders. That means the long-term future is often sacrificed for short-term gains – leading to job insecurity, underinvestment and the increasing dominance of mergers, acquisitions and sell-offs. This is a fairly unsatisfactory way to run businesses; it would seem a disastrous model for running the country.

The second problem with the IKEA argument is that it is would be a massive – indeed possibly fatal – blow to the democratic ideal. If we were to let IKEA managers 'run the country' what would we be essentially saying? That they take over all the functions of public administrators? Or that they take over the functions of parliament or the president altogether? If so, to whom would they be accountable? For whom would they be running the country? Who would set their agenda? Indeed, what on earth would they running?

If they are to remain IKEA managers in nature (highly unlikely), then they'd be running the country simply as a business to maximise profits for shareholders. That could simply mean milking the country and all its people dry to bring dividends to outside shareholders. Naturally, they'd want to cut dead wood from the business: children, old people, pregnant mothers, the sick and poorly trained, the slow, the unnecessary, those who might want to rock the boat, the wild birds and animals, the unproductive woodlands and riverbanks – indeed anyone or anything that doesn't directly contribute to the labour force or productivity. A country is a community, and cannot be run as a profit-making business. But the problem is if we gave the country over to IKEA managers, we'd have no way to stop them doing this. They become utterly unaccountable, and the country is in effect a tyranny. Mussolini and Hitler both justified their actions by saying they were running the country well. Who's to say IKEA managers wouldn't claim the same?

Running a country is about so much more than making a profit. It's about looking after its people. It's about making sure we all have the chance of a decent life, a decent home, food, care in sickness, proper education, justice and security, freedom of speech, protection of the fabric and heritage of the country for the benefit of all, and so much more. None of these come into making a profit at all – and for all these we need politicians not retail managers.

For all its flaws, true democracy is by far the best way of government anyone has yet thought of. But democracy requires democratic representatives and our participation in the process. We cannot simply hand over the functions of government, without handing over our democratic system and our control over the way the country is. Democracy requires either direct participation or elected representatives, that is, politicians. If we cannot trust the incumbent politicians to run the country, we cannot simply abandon the idea of representation – we need to find politicians who we can trust. And then of course, there will be those tiresome weekends struggling to assemble your statutory government quota of flat-pack furniture …

Here is a piece of bark, please talk about it (Biological Sciences, Oxford)

Every kind of tree has its own unique bark pattern that an expert can identify as easily as leaves. The papery white of silver birch is unmistakable. But from the grey colour and rough texture, with those deep ski-run fissures and oblong scales, I'd guess this bark is some species of oak.

Bark is a tree's guard against the world – its shield against the weather and its defence from natural predators that would damage the vulnerable tissues inside. Life is a wonderful, precious thing – a tiny realm of order in the vast chaos of the unliving universe around – and all living things need protection. A cell has its cytoplasm. Fish have their scales. Humans have skin. Bark is a tree's.

Without bark, trees could never grow so tall nor endure so long. Many trees can live for centuries, surviving winter chill or summer heat, drought, flood and fire, as well as the unwanted attention of insects, fungi and many other pests. While herbaceous plants – green plants without bark – must forever be growing anew and spreading, trees can send up a single trunk that lives on year after year, protected by bark.

Thick bark like oak bark is particularly effective protection. Its toughness protects the softer, living part of the tree from animals like deer that might gnaw on it, while tannins and other chemicals in the bark deter destructive insects. The bark's air-filled cells and moisture content insulate the inner wood against warm and cold, while its ridges and scales not only trap insulating air, but also become radiator fins, and so reduce temperature variations. In dry, fire-prone regions, thick bark shields a tree against the heat of all but the most intense blazes. Smooth bark, like beech, protects in a different way. It offers far less insulation and armour, but its smoothness makes it much harder for insects and plants such as epiphytes to get a grip, which is why smooth bark is the norm in tropical regions.

Yet bark is much more than just a tree's armour. Beneath the dry, dark and dead corky material of the outer bark, there is a multi-layered sandwich of paler, living tissues, known collectively as the periderm. Innermost there's the softish 'active phloem' through which are piped the fluids that carry the sugars and nutrients the tree needs to grow. Outside the phloem there's another couple of layers: the cork skin and the cork cambium.

The cork cambium is where the cork cells grow that in time die and form the outer cork shell of the bark. The cork skin is the greenness you see when bark is just stripped and still living – green because it contains the pigment chlorophyll. It's not just a tree's leaves that catch the sun's energy in photosynthesis; these green bark cells do a little photosynthesising too – the thinner the bark, the more they can do. When leaves fall in winter, bark cells add energy to help the tree through.

Each year a tree grows by adding phloem cells just under the bark. That's what creates the yearly growth rings. By the end of the year, some phloem cells have been squeezed out to form the cork cambium, then die and become the outside of the bark. As the tree's girth swells, thick bark like oak cracks into wonderfully gnarled ridges and furrows to accommodate the growth. Smooth bark like beech grows slower and expands without cracking, so beech trees may sometimes still bear witness centuries later to a name carved into the bark on romantic impulse.

Humans aren't the only ones to make their mark on bark. For beavers, of course, bark is breakfast. Quite a few voles dine on it too, while woodpeckers cling on and hammer into it to get at bark beetles, termites, spiders and ants, and treecreepers shimmy up and down searching for insects in its nooks and crannies. In fact, bark is a little wildlife habitat in its own right, mottled green with variegated mosses and lichens; crawling with and burrowed by myriad insects and other tiny creatures. Even when dead and lying on the forest floor, bark is a rich habitat for fungi and insects and other bugs.

It has a range of uses for us too. Long ago, native North Americans made canoes out of paper birch bark, native Australians made shelters and natives in

South America made clothes. Today, of course, cork bark gives us cork, and the latex fluid in rubber tree bark gives us rubber. And bark can be medicinal, too. Aspirin, for instance, came originally from the bark of the willow tree, and the phenolics in Scots pine may help treat arthritis.

Unlike the showy green of leaves, bark is mostly browns and greys, and blends into the soft, intense dun-ness of woods and forests with an unobtrusiveness that only emphasises the deep and subtle richness of its hues and textures, and provides a ground for all the other colours of the wood to glow. It's easy to forget the bark for the trees, but when you look at bark closely, it reveals itself as a substance of breathtaking beauty – not just in its appearance and feel, but in the perfection with which it performs its allotted natural function of protecting the tree throughout its life.

My little girl says she knows she's going to get a brother when my wife gives birth in seven months' time. Is she right? *(Maths, Cambridge)*

This is a maths question, so we're going to assume that the little girl isn't clairvoyant – and of course it's too early in the pregnancy for an ultrasound scan. So how could the little girl know if the new baby will be a boy? The immediate answer might be that she can't; the baby could equally well be a girl or a boy.

But the question is actually a sly allusion to a well-known conundrum in elementary probability theory, known as the boy–girl problem. This asks: if there is a family with two children, and one is a boy, is the other child a girl or a boy? Intuitively, you'd say that since roughly half of all children are boys and half are girls, it could be either. But this, some claim, is where probabilities surprise expectations.

The balance of probabilities, the argument goes, means that the other child is a girl. The odds are apparently two to one in favour, for reasons I'll come back to. Even though there is a roughly even chance that any single child will be a boy or a girl, the picture changes when there are two children involved to give a counter-intuitive answer, revealing an answer you might not expect to know.

The mathematics of probability is one of the big

breakthroughs of the 20th century and has had an enormous impact on our lives. Its importance is in providing tools for studying – and even predicting – random, chance or multiple disconnected events. Through its applied branch of statistics it comes into things as diverse as forecasting the weather and predicting floods to calculating the safety of new drugs or the fluctuations of the financial market.

Traditional maths, like the maths of Newton, is the maths of certainty, about the regular patterns in nature. Probability maths is the maths of uncertainty, about the irregularities of nature. Jacob Bernoulli summed it up brilliantly as 'the art of conjecture' back in 1713:

> We define the art of conjecture, or stochastic art, as the art of evaluating as exactly as possible the probabilities of things, so that in our judgements and actions we can always base ourselves on what has been found to be the best, the most appropriate, the most certain, the best advised; this is the only object of the wisdom of the philosopher and the prudence of the statesmen.

Probability maths is a remarkable and much more precise way of doing what we do naturally all the time – try to make sense of the world, spot patterns, notice similarities and differences, regularities and irregularities. It's how we find things that might threaten us, or that can be used to improve things.

At its very simplest, it's about the odds of a coin landing heads or tails, of you rolling a double six three times in a row (hugely against). At its most sophisticated, it's about plotting models of how global climate will change if carbon emissions rise unchecked – or even the chances of other universes existing for us to escape into if it gets too hot here.

What is so valuable about probability maths is that it provides tools for guessing what is likely to happen in the future from what has happened in the past, or in different circumstances. It doesn't provide a certain outcome, but a probability is an immense help in the real world. It dramatically strengthens the effectiveness of our choices.

So can probability theory help our questioner's baby prediction? In the simple boy–girl conundrum, the probabilities are sometimes said to give the answer in the following way. If we know one of the children in a two-child family is a girl, then the girl's sibling is apparently most likely to be a brother. In any two-child family, these are the four possibilities:

Girl–girl
Boy–girl
Girl–boy
Boy–boy

Since one child is a little girl, that rules out the

boy–boy combination. That leaves three other possible combinations:

Girl–girl
Girl–boy
Boy–girl

In only one of the three possibilities is the second child a girl, it seems. In other words, in a two-child family, the unknown child is twice as likely to be of the opposite gender.

The baby prediction, however, throws into the spotlight the flaws in this way of thinking – and how easy it can be to misapply probabilities. On the face of it, the precocious little girl might know that because she is a girl the logic of the boy–girl conundrum means she is right to expect a baby brother. In fact, a moment's thought makes it clear that there are only two possible outcomes – the baby will be a boy or it will be a girl – not three. So the odds on either are even and the questioner's little girl cannot tell the future using probabilities in this way.

So what is the flaw in the thinking in the boy–girl conundrum? It's in regarding boy–girl and girl–boy as two possibilities, not one. In fact, it's only two if the question is presented in an especially contrived way, where placing in the family matters as well as gender.

But is there anything in population demographics

instead which might indicate a sex bias in particular families that might enable a prediction? Are families more often single sex or mixed? Instances of single sex families are very striking, so it's very tempting to assume there might be a pattern, with some families genetically disposed to producing girls and others boys. My mother was one of a family of six girls, and I myself have two brothers and no sisters. So are second children more likely to be the same gender as the first? An extensive study of US families between 1970 and 2000 by Joseph Lee Rodgers and Debby Doughty showed this isn't so. In the study, all-girl families were very marginally less numerous than all-boy or boy–girl/ girl–boy families, but not to any statistically significant degree. The same is true of third children. There is no statistical evidence for gender bias at all.

In our attempt to make sense of the world and spot patterns – to guess probabilities – we are apt to read more into striking incidents and coincidences than is necessarily justified. Indeed, it's such a strong temptation that even presented with the statistical evidence to the contrary, many will still assert that the statistics are wrong in their own particular case.

In the meantime, the questioner's little girl will have to wait for the first ultrasound next month – or maybe longer – to discover if the power of her positive thinking will bring the baby brother she hopes for. Maybe she's right …

If a wife had expressed distaste for it previously, would her husband's habit of putting marmalade in his egg at breakfast be grounds for divorce?

(Law, Cambridge)

What a wonderfully comic scenario! You can just see the pained look in the coutured wife's eyes as she tries to sip her Kenco filter coffee while her husband defiantly smears a dollop of marmalade on to his egg before wiping his fingers on his shabby old pullover. Classic BBC sitcom. Hardly grounds for divorce, more for a comedy award.

Yet despite the comedy, it is often what to the observer seem comically trivial differences like this that the real pain of a marriage may turn on. Such small events can have a symbolism for the couple that cuts very deep, and the scenario may actually be more Madame Bovary than Mrs Bucket.

For the wife, the husband's odd behaviour may be a repeated dagger to the heart of the wrong choice she has made, and the fact that he can't respond to her quite reasonable plea to forgo even this small eccentricity for her sake positively cruel.

Fortunately, we have largely moved on from the days when a wife could never get a divorce from her husband no matter how cruel or abusive, and when she was so much her husband's slave that even rape and physical abuse could go on legally within a marriage. Society has recognised that marriages do break down irretrievably and couples must be able to make the separation legally as well as physically.

But this question of the marmalade egg, in all its apparent absurdity, homes in on the strange and ambiguous place in law occupied by divorce. The fact is that in most countries 'grounds' are needed for divorce. Although divorce laws vary from country to country, a partner cannot usually end a marriage legally simply by saying 'It's over', even if the emotional impact of such a declaration is clear.

The UK adopts a particularly traditional line in this. Most US states (except for New York) and most European countries now have a 'no fault' avenue for divorce, enabling couples to divorce by mutual consent. The UK toyed with the idea of introducing 'no fault' divorce as part of the Family Law Act introduced in 1996 by the John Major government. But a long campaign by the *Daily Mail* and others led to it being dropped by the incoming Tony Blair government.

The campaigners argued that having no-fault divorce undermined the institution of marriage and stopped people from working to save their union by 'letting them off' too easily. Tory Lords leader Baroness Young said at the time, 'No-fault divorce lowers marriage to something of less value than a television licence. There would be no punishment for breaking a marriage, whether you made a promise in church or a contract in a register office. But if you don't pay for a television licence you can go to jail.' One can't be sure whether she was arguing for TV licence offenders to be let off, or for divorcees to be sent to jail or worse for their heinous crime, but arguments like these won the day, and so the UK still has, exceptionally, no procedure for divorce that does not involve blame. The only ground for divorce with no fault is two years' separation by consent – and the consent is only valid if agreed in writing.

Baroness Young's comment that breaking a marriage should be 'punished' highlights the legal absurdities entailed in marriage and divorce. Can you look at marriage wholly as a legal contract for which there should be penalties for breaking? Currently marriage is indeed viewed by the law as a legal contract, and it must therefore go through a court procedure to be terminated. But it has long been recognised by lawyers as a highly anomalous one.

The problem is that it is impossible to legally prescribe all the obligations and expectations between people in a marriage. Couples promise to love each other in their marriage vows, for instance, but that can hardly be made a binding legal obligation! Although some people do draw up detailed prenuptial contracts, most wed perfectly happily without them – and even where there are contracts they rarely cover the things that lead to divorce in most cases; they simply make the separation of possessions after the marriage has failed more clear-cut.

So marriage is a very odd kind of contract. As Canadian philosopher Will Kymlicka says, 'there is no written document, each party gives up its right to self-protection, the terms of the contract cannot be re-negotiated, neither party need understand its terms, it must be between two and only two people.'

Indeed, treating marriage as a contract that can only be terminated through a judicial procedure in the courts is surely flawed. Really, it is a hangover from the days when the legal side did matter, when a wife did become her husband's legal possession. Fortunately, those days are long gone, and marriage is seen in most parts of the world simply as a mutual agreement between two consenting adults. Fortunately, too, the idea that divorce is shameful and that one partner needed to prove their innocence is largely a thing of the past. And happily, the days when one of the couple thought it appropriate to fight in court to prevent the marriage break-up are mostly gone, too.

Yet in the UK divorce remains a judicial matter in which, in theory, parties have to apportion blame and find 'grounds' for divorce, rather than a simple civil administrative procedure. Of course, the legal system is well aware that times have moved on and in practice the proof needed to demonstrate blame is small. In reality, it is only a little harder for couples to divorce in the UK by mutual consent than in countries that have 'no fault' divorce.

If then, the idea of finding grounds for divorce is largely specious, then it hardly matters how valid the grounds are. So in many ways the fact that the wife considers her husband's marmalade misdemeanour grounds for divorce should be enough for the divorce to be granted, whatever anybody else's opinion. It should be the couple's decision that matters, not the court's. It seems absurd that the court should play any part whatsoever in deciding grounds for divorce; only the couple themselves can truly know if their marriage is over.

In other words, it's my opinion that marmalade eggs, toasty fingers the wrong way up, sausages and jam or any kind of trivial irritation should be admissible as grounds for divorce. It doesn't mean that any old triviality is enough *reason* to break a marriage, but they should be enough legal grounds.

However much we want to support the idea of marriage, however much we want all marriages to survive, however much we want couples to strive to find a way past their difficulties and stay together, we surely must acknowledge that the courts really should have no part to play in that process. The law should only be involved to settle disputes and look after the interests of other parties, such as children.

If the marmalade egg case did come up in a divorce court, it might be considered by the court grounds for divorce or might not be. You'd have to know much more of the story to guess the verdict, to see whether it was just an irritation or part of a pattern of mental cruelty. I for one would love to hear more of that story.

Which way is the Earth spinning? (Natural
Sciences, Cambridge)

It all depends on how you look at it.* It spins eastwards, of course, which is why the sun comes up in the east

---

* You could just say it's spinning my way – because any description of motion depends entirely on the frame of reference. The only easily visible signs that the Earth is spinning are the daily movement of the sun and stars through the sky, and the sun's shifting shadows on the ground. Yet we have so little sensation of movement it's no wonder that for a long time most people thought just the sun and the stars moved while the Earth was forever fixed. Even now, it's not always easy to remember as you watch the sun sink below the horizon in the west that it's really the Earth and you moving, not the sun.

Some clever Ancient Greek astronomers such as Aristarchus guessed that the Earth spins over 2,000 years ago. Yet the clues that it is spinning are so subtle that they were not really picked up until the 16th century when Polish astronomer Copernicus introduced to Europe the idea that the Earth orbits the sun. Even then, a century on, Galileo was drawn into ferocious battles that ended in his house arrest when he tried to make the case for a moving Earth in the face of official opposition from the Catholic church. It's easy for us, four centuries on, to ridicule the church elders who abused Galileo – but his evidence that the Earth moves amounted to little more than the observation of moonlike phases on Venus through a telescope added to Copernicus's ingenious (and correct) interpretation of the loops in the tracks of the planets through the sky. After Galileo, Newton and others tried with little success to detect the Earth's motion in the deflection from the vertical of falling objects. But it wasn't until 1851 that French physicist Léon Foucault was able to provide clear evidence of Earth's motion with his pendulum, which slowly shifts the direction it swings during the day as the Earth rotates while its momentum carries in the same direction. Nowadays, of course, we are finally able to move beyond the Earth and witness its rotation from the outside, from space.

and sinks in the west as the Earth whirls us away out of sight of it. And if you travel far out into space above the North Pole, you might also say it spins anticlockwise.

Astronomers might then go a little further and describe Earth's rotation as 'prograde'. Prograde simply means turning in the same direction (retrograde means turning in the opposite direction). So when they say Earth's rotation is prograde, they are saying that it is spinning on its axis in the same direction as it is orbiting around the sun. It's as if the Earth is rolling forever forward as it journeys through space. In fact, most of the planets in the solar system spin the same way. The only exceptions are Venus and Uranus, which spin slowly backwards.

Strikingly, not just the rotation but also the 'revolution' or orbit of all the planets, including Venus and Uranus, is prograde. That means they all orbit the sun in the same way the sun is turning, too. In fact, pretty much everything in the solar system is spinning the same way. Even moons orbit their planets in the same way. And now as astronomers discover other planetary systems circling other stars, they are finding that these planets mostly turn the same way as their stars as well, although there are exceptions. So prograde motion seems to rule, despite the odd rebel.*

---

* Actually it's not just planets, stars and galaxies that are on the whirl. A fascinating study by a team led by Michael Longo at the University of Michigan recently looked at the direction of rotation

Astronomers have been aware of this widespread tendency to prograde motion in the solar system for several centuries. It was in trying to explain it that thinkers such as Kant and Laplace developed the nebular hypothesis of how the solar system came into being in the later 1700s. There are numerous theories about the origins of the solar system, but the nebular hypothesis is still the most widely accepted.

In the nebular hypothesis, the solar system began as a huge gas cloud or nebula. Perhaps triggered by a collision with another cloud, or by a star exploding nearby, it began to collapse inwards under the force of its own gravity. As it contracted, the material gained what is called angular momentum.

Angular momentum is a hugely important quality in the motion of space. In fact, it's why everything in space seems to whirl around like some infinitely vast clockwork toy. Everything in motion has momentum, the natural tendency to carry on moving in the same direction. Angular momentum is momentum in a circle, and occurs whenever the direction of momentum is pulled continuously off course by some additional

---

of over 15,000 spiral galaxies in the part of the sky towards the north pole of the Milky Way. What they found was that significantly more are rotating anticlockwise than clockwise. If more galaxies do spin in this direction, Longo argues, then the universe must have a net anticlockwise angular momentum. Since that momentum must have come from somewhere, it implies the universe was born spinning.

force. In space, that force is mostly gravity. Wherever there is gravity and motion, which is essentially everywhere, gravity turns motion into angular momentum. So circular motion is universal. Angular momentum is what makes the Milky Way and other galaxies turn, the solar system rotate, and planets and moons orbit. It's also what makes the Earth spin.

The key thing to remember about angular momentum is that, like linear momentum, it can't just get lost; it is always conserved. In the nebular hypothesis, any slight rotation the original cloud had was magnified as it collapsed. Its angular momentum was packed into a smaller and smaller space so that it began to spin ever faster.* There is a famous analogy about the conservation of angular momentum with a spinning skater. As she tucks her arms in, the concentration of momentum means she spins faster. So it was with the infant solar system.

With the nebular hypothesis, a cloud perhaps a light-year across was reduced to the size of the solar system. So there's a lot of momentum to pack into a tiny space, and the collapse of the nebula was like winding up a giant clockwork toy. As the original ball of the cloud collapsed, so its matter was concentrated and flung out in a flat, spinning pancake disc. Then,

---

* With neutron stars the gravitational collapse is so dramatic and the concentration of angular momentum so huge that these tiny stars can spin up to 642 times a second!

as gravity pulled material in the disc together to form planets, all the momentum of the vast original cloud was concentrated into spinning them like tops.

That original momentum was enough to keep the Earth spinning relentlessly at the same speed far into the future. There are small frictional forces, known as tidal forces, caused by the gravitational interaction between the Earth, moon and sun that act as brakes. But they slow it down by barely 2.3 milliseconds per day every hundred years. Weather systems in the atmosphere can be a drag on the planet and affect the speed of the spin, too. Earthquakes can actually speed the Earth up or slow it down by shifting its mass. The quake that struck Japan in 2011 apparently accelerated the Earth's rotation and shortened the day by 1.8 microseconds by shifting mass towards the equator.

I've talked about the speed of Earth's spin as if it's the same everywhere. This is not quite true. If you stand right on the poles, for instance, it takes you a whole day to turn right round, but you're not moving any distance. Yet if you stand on the equator, you're whirled round at 1,667km/h – faster than the speed of sound. That's why spacecraft are often launched from tropical locations, to give them extra launch speed.

If you go down into the Earth's interior, too, the speed varies. This is because the centre of the Earth is fluid and magnetic. The spinning of the magnetic material in the Earth's core creates a magnetic field, and this in turn affects the metal in the core. It pushes the inner core eastwards, making it spin faster than the rest of the Earth, and it pushes the fluid outer core in the opposite direction so that it actually turns westwards relative to the rest of the Earth.

In talking about the way the Earth spins, I've talked so far about the direction it spins. But I could also talk about how it spins. From the geometry of our view of the sun and planets, we know that the Earth doesn't spin perpendicular to its orbit around the sun but at a slight angle. Its axis, which runs in a line between the North Pole and the South Pole, is tilted over at an average of 23.4° to the plane of the orbit. This tilt is why we get seasons, since it ensures that as Earth moves through its orbit, the direct line of sun strikes at different places.

In fact, the way the Earth spins varies continually. Over a 42,000-year cycle, for instance, its spin axis wobbles a little between 22.1° and 24.5°. Over 26,000 years, too, the axis moves slowly round in a circle, tracing out a cone, in a movement called precession. And over just eighteen to nineteen years, a tiny wobble called nutation is superimposed on the precession because Earth's equator is not perfectly aligned with the moon, making the rotation slightly unbalanced by the pull of their mutual gravity. Serbian mathematician Milutin Milankovitch showed how these variations might alter the warming power of the sun and create variations in climate, now called Milankovitch cycles.

In the 1978 movie, Superman used his super-strength to reverse the spin of the Earth to turn back time and save Lois Lane. Maybe some other force will one day intervene and change the rotation of the Earth. But until then, we can be certain the sun will rise in the east and set in the west, and that's how it should be.

Should we have laws for the use of light bulbs? (Law, Cambridge)

Climate change is throwing up some tricky dilemmas for liberal-minded people, and this is one of them. The big problem is that climate change is a global problem that purely individual behaviour doesn't seem to be able to solve. Economists would say it's a case of 'market failure' because people acting in their own self-interest seem incapable of dealing with the problem.

Scientists are in little doubt about the vital and urgent need to cut emissions of greenhouse gases, carbon dioxide especially. But since individuals and a free market have singularly failed, it's very clear that consensus and concerted official action are needed to make any headway. In other words, if we are to avoid potential disaster on a global scale, we have to accept that governments need to take control measures to limit carbon emissions. And yet, if governments are taking action to control carbon then they are, inevitably, restricting someone's freedom to use it. This is why climate control measures are proving so slow to make progress and are so mired in controversy.

The question 'Should we have laws for the use of light bulbs?' encapsulates this issue in a nutshell. Anxious to find ways of reducing carbon emissions, an array of governments around the world decided in 2007 to focus, interestingly, on light bulbs. National governments, from Australia to the USA, introduced legislation to restrict the use of 'wasteful' incandescent light bulbs.

It is not entirely clear why, of all the things they could have done, they decided that this particular measure should be the subject of one of the first pieces of coordinated legal action on climate change. It probably seemed like an easy bit of action to take because there was no obvious pain involved. The public wasn't being asked to cut down on anything, or pay extra; all they had to do was change the kind of light bulb they used when they bought a new one. So no government presumably expected to face much criticism or opposition – and could claim kudos for doing something to deal with climate change.

Yet as it turned out, even this 'safe' piece of legislation quickly sparked a controversy that has not gone away. It was all very well banning the sale of incandescent bulbs, but there was not a perfect 'energy-saving' bulb to replace it. Incandescent bulbs may use a lot of energy, but they are or were cheap and produced a warm, cosy and bright glow at the flick of a switch.

The most obvious alternative – CFL (compact fluorescent bulbs), which curl a fluorescent tube up into the shape of a conventional light bulb – fail on all these counts. They are more expensive, very slow to warm up – and don't work at all in cold conditions – and they emit a discontinuous spectrum of colours which many people find harsh and unpleasant. The slight flicker of CFLs gives some people migraine and headaches. And to cap it all, their mercury content makes them environmentally hazardous to dispose of, and mildly dangerous to health if broken in use.

Mostly, though, it was the ugly light that offended. The warm glow of incandescent bulbs is crucial to how many people feel about their homes, the way they arrange their light to create the right ambience. It's a reminder of the primeval comfort of the tribal fire – and this enforced change to bright white artificial bulbs seemed an intrusion on people's personal, intimate space. Not everyone felt like this, of course, but many became rebels on the quiet, stockpiling huge supplies of the old incandescent bulbs – ordinary law-abiding people secretly stepping outside the law to protect their personal way of life.

In the UK, as the ban approached, letters and leaders flooded the media protesting against this draconian piece of lawmaking by faceless European Union bureaucrats. (In fact, it was the UK that pushed for the legislation and led the way in Europe.)

The immediate controversy seems to have died down for a while as people used these stockpiles to keep the golden glow of incandescent alight in their homes. But the question of whether such laws as this are justified or right remains a key issue as the issue of what to do to deal with climate change gathers momentum.

Light bulb laws are a restriction of your liberty – an intrusion, many would say, upon your right to choose how you live your life in your own home. So are laws like this an unwarranted attack on personal liberty or not? The great philosopher John Locke, who set the tone for much English thinking about the law argued that they are not. Central to Locke's thinking is the idea that laws serve to protect freedom, not curb it. Laws are intended not to abolish or restrain freedom but protect and enlarge it. 'Freedom is not,' Locke says, 'liberty for every man to do as he lists (for who could be free when every other man's humour might domineer over him?)'.

In light of Locke's reasoning, the argument that it is your right to choose which kind of light to use in your own home falls down quickly. You only have a right to choose entirely freely if your choice has no impact on others. Otherwise, your freedom must be mediated to protect the freedom of others. Restrictions on your choice of light bulbs may be necessary to give the next generation the freedom to simply breathe. Interestingly, though, the ban on incandescent bulbs in most countries was applied only to the manufacture and sale of the bulbs, not the use – so you can still choose to use them if you wish, if you can find them.

Laws are vital to protect the freedom of all. Indeed, as Locke said, 'Where there is no law there is no freedom'. So in principle there should be no problem with laws on the use of light bulbs if they help preserve the freedom of the next generation to live a tolerable life. The dilemma, however, is whether they do. Not all laws preserve freedom. Bad laws, even if well intentioned, can have a negative impact.

My own personal instinct is that the incandescent light bulb ban was not a good law. I am not convinced it will significantly reduce energy consumption, by the time all the various other factors are brought into play – and I am convinced that it will significantly impair the look and feel of many homes. It has the feeling of an easy measure by which governments are seen to be doing something, rather than actually doing something – a way of avoiding making the really difficult choices.

Dealing with climate change is posing the world a moral dilemma on a massive scale. It is plain that changes need to be urgently made to cut energy consumption and the emission of greenhouse gases. It is also plain that individuals may not make these changes of their own volition – or rather, not enough individuals will change, or change sufficiently.

So the process must be guided by regulations. But how do we decide on the necessary regulations in the face of so many conflicting interests? Is it right, for instance, to impose cuts on the use of fossil fuels on developing countries, when the lion's share of the gases now in the atmosphere came from the developed countries which gained their riches by using these fuels in huge amounts? We are going to have to make some choices, and soon – and light bulbs are just one aspect of the changes that may be needed.

What do you think of teleport machines? *(Economics and Management, Oxford)*

Ever since Captain Kirk uttered the immortal words, 'Beam me up, Scotty' in the TV science fiction series *Star Trek* back in the 1970s, the idea of teleportation has been firmly in the public consciousness. Teleport machines are the ultimate sci-fi fantasy trip. Why squash yourself into the commuter train from Balham when you can live in Hawaii and teleport to work in the blink of an eye? Why settle for the pleasures of the local ice rink when you can beam yourself off to skate on the ice oceans of Titan?

The amazing thing is that, far-fetched though these human space-hops seem, teleportation machines are not science fiction; they are science fact, and have been for a few decades now.

It all began with Albert Einstein's understandable scepticism about the uncertainty at the heart of quantum ideas. Einstein just couldn't relate to a universe directed by probability; it just didn't seem scientific. 'God doesn't play dice,' he apocryphally said, and he devised a thought experiment to prove quantum theory wrong. In this experiment, known as the Einstein–Podolsky–Rosen (EPR) experiment, a pair of particles is emitted simultaneously from an atom.

Einstein played with quantum theory's insistence that things only become fixed once they are observed.

So, he said, the 'spin' of the two emitted particles is not fixed until they are actually observed, and yet the instant one of them is observed and fixed then the other's spin must be fixed too – even if it is on the other side of the universe.

Absurd, eh? thought Einstein. So quantum theory must be wrong. Then in 1982, amazingly, French physicist Alain Aspect showed that the EPR is a real effect. The two particles are said to be 'entangled'. It's as if they are twins that can telepathically communicate across space.

Amazingly, too, entanglement has been demonstrated again and again over the last few decades and it's the basis for real, working teleportation machines.

The idea is that if you attach another particle to one of an entangled pair, the attachment is instantly recreated, seemingly magically, in the other one of the pair – no matter how far apart. In 1997, photons were teleported across a laboratory in Rome like this, and since then molecules as big as bacteria have been teleported. In 2012, Chinese scientists managed to teleport a photon 97km in an instant. And in 2013, Swiss scientists succeeded in teleporting data through an electronic circuit.

So teleporting machines are real, and I find them astounding. There is no way humans are going to be transported soon in the *Star Trek* way, however, despite the progress. The amount of data to be transferred in beaming a human is massive. Some physics students recently calculated that teleporting the data to rebuild the trillion trillion (that is, 10^{24}) atoms in a human being would take 350,000 times as long as the universe is old! And there is another problem. All current thinking about teleportation doesn't actually move the object – it destroys it and recreates it in another place. So to teleport me from here to Havana, you'd have to vaporise me here to recreate me in Havana. Quite apart from the existential and philosophical crisis this might bring upon me – is the Havana me really me? – I'm not sure I relish the idea of being turned to dust continually or even once.

And if teleporting does not actually move you but recreate you in another place, then the idea is less distinctive than it first seems. A conversation on Skype, for instance, creates an instant visual and audio version of you in another place without destroying the original you – and it doesn't require much imagination to see that in the future, the input from the Skype version that feeds back to you could be enhanced just a little so that it is becoming so remarkably close to being there it will almost be as if you were teleported.

Similarly the idea of avatars in virtual space is becoming more and more commonplace and developed, and of course some thinkers have toyed with the idea of uploading all our thoughts so that we exist in cyberspace independently of our bodies. If that happens, human teleport machines become rather tame and redundant – long before they become a reality.

Nonetheless, the 'modest' particle shifting teleport machines have already achieved is among the most remarkable scientific achievements of the age. First of all, the fact such machines even work at any level is stunning confirmation of quantum theory – a both disturbing (as it was for Einstein) and thrilling confirmation that we live, at some level, in a shifting, enigmatic universe that works not deterministically but on probability. There is something a little unnerving about particles disappearing in one place and popping up in another, but if this is really how the universe works – and it seems that it does – maybe it will help open our minds to new possibilities, and new ways of looking at reality.

Everyday technology has already shown what can be done in small ways by adjusting to the new reality of the quantum. Computer flash drives, for instance, exploit the quantum phenomenon of tunnelling, which enables particles to 'jump' instantaneously from one side of a barrier to another. Could teleport machine concepts be developed in ways that will bring us an array of different technologies that can't yet be foreseen? It seems highly likely. Already scientists are developing teleporting ideas that can transmit data, which may be developed into computers of a completely different power and speed to those of today.

In the meantime, I have no need to wait for scientists of the future to build a teleport machine to beam me across the other side of the universe, or take me on an instant trip to Hawaii. I have a teleport machine right here in my head. It's called my imagination. It's cheap to run, on tap all the time – and what's more it allows me to shape my destination as well as my arrival. Sometimes I need a book, or a film, or a piece of music to trigger it – or an Oxbridge tutor's interview question – but it's there.

How many molecules are there in a glass of water? (Natural Sciences, Cambridge)

A lot, is the simple answer. Molecules are so tiny and there are likely to be so many in a glass of water that it would be impossible to count them directly. So I'm going to have to come at the answer indirectly. In fact, the calculation is fairly simple, and the reason this is so takes us back to the very foundations of chemistry, and the first beginnings of the atomic theory of matter.

Indeed, it's all down to a flash of insight by the man some called the father of chemistry, John Dalton. Back in the late 1700s, scientists knew about atoms but thought they were all the same size, and hadn't quite twigged that each element has its own unique atom. While Dalton was doing some experiments with the gases of the air, he was surprised to see that pure oxygen will not absorb as much water vapour as pure nitrogen. He guessed that this is because oxygen atoms are bigger and heavier than nitrogen atoms, so leave less room. If this first guess was brilliant, his next was sheer genius.

The identity of atoms was all about weight ratios! And from that moment, weights have been at the heart of atomic and molecular chemistry – and they're going to be the way to count our glassful of molecules.

Atoms are the 'ultimate particles' of each element, Dalton saw, and they combine to make compounds in very simple ratios. If that is so, he could work out the relative weight of an atom of any element just by measuring the total weight of the element involved in a compound. Simple and effective. Soon he'd worked out the relative atomic weights of each element then known.

He used hydrogen as a base, since it is the lightest gas, and gave it an atomic weight of 1. Because the amount of oxygen in water is seven times heavier than the amount of hydrogen, Dalton assigned oxygen an atomic weight of 7. Equally simple – or so he thought (it's actually 16, or thereabouts).

Unfortunately, there was a flaw in Dalton's method; he didn't realise that atoms of the same element can combine. He always assumed that a compound of atoms, a molecule, had only one atom of each element. Of course, he was wrong.

This is where a near contemporary of Dalton's comes in – probably very slowly, since his name is absurdly long and grand: Lorenzo Romano Amedeo Carlo Avogadro di Quaregna e di Cerreto. Avogadro, as he's usually known, was an aristocratic Italian scientist. It had already been shown by Gay-Lussac that when two gases react together to form a third, they always combine in simple whole-number ratios. But for this to be true, Avogadro realised, equal volumes of any two gases at the same temperature and pressure must hold an equal number of particles. If so, then the ratios must mean a molecule can combine varying numbers of atoms. What matters in working out ratios, then, is molecular proportions. Over the next half-century, scientists realised that Avogadro's idea of using molecular proportions would allow them to calculate atomic weights correctly.

Avogadro went on to show that equal volumes of a gas (at a given temperature and pressure) always contain an equal number of atoms or molecules. In other words, the relationship between volume and the particle number is always the same, and since 1909 it's been called Avogadro's constant.

What Avogadro's constant does is tell us how many particles there are in a particular amount of a substance. The numbers involved, of course, are so huge and unmanageable that a special unit has been devised for this: the mole (a word which owes its origin to molecules, not infiltrators or blind burrowers).

Although Avogadro came up with the principle in the early 1800s, it wasn't until 1910 that Robert Millikan was finally able to give a number to the mole. In the same way as I will with our glassful of molecules, Millikan came at it indirectly. He simply measured the total electric charge in a particular mass of carbon-12 then divided it by the recently discovered charge on a single electron. That way he could work out how many electrons the mass contained. The numbers were of course absolutely gigantic. In every 12g of carbon-12, there are 6.022×10^{23} atoms! Some very keen chemists celebrate 10/23 (23 October) as Mole Day every year ...

The number has since been refined,* but that figure will do for my estimate. A mole is the amount of a substance that contains this number of particles, whether it be molecules, electrons or atoms. Since the atomic mass of hydrogen is about 1, a twelfth that of carbon-12, it contains this number of particles in just a twelfth of this mass – that is, 1g. A mole of hydrogen is 1g. Oxygen has an atomic mass of about 16, so a mole of oxygen is 16g. So a mole of water, H_2O, its molecular mass, is 1g + 1g + 16g, that is, 18g.

So the key to my calculations is mass, as it was with John Dalton two centuries ago. I can't count the molecules in a glass of water, but I can have a good guess at the water's mass. I'm going to guess that there's a fifth of a litre of water in the glass – so 200g of water.

Since the molecular mass of water is 18g, this means the glass contains just over eleven moles (200 divided by 18). So there you have it: there are approximately 11 $\times$ 6.022 $\times$ 10^{23} or 6.624 $\times$ 10^{24} molecules in a glass of water. That's just about 6 trillion trillion.

This is only an approximate figure of course, but the method works, and if I was able to measure the weight of water accurately and used the very precise figures for atomic weights now known, I could work out the number of molecules in a glass precisely. And I was right first time. It's a lot …

---

* 6.02214129(27) $\times$ 10^{23}

How is it possible that a sailing boat can go faster than the wind? *(Engineering, Oxford)*

Well my first instinct might be to say, this is a trick question: it isn't possible. A log carried down by a river can't possibly go faster than the current. So how could a sailing boat possibly go faster than the wind pushing it? That's common sense, surely? You can't fool me! Of course I could be 'clever' and say 'with an outboard motor', or 'on the back of a lorry'. But those glib and tricksy answers are rarely interesting for more than a second or two.

And if you think again about how sailing boats work, you may realise that common sense doesn't always give you the right answer either. Some of the greatest scientific breakthroughs have been made when some genius finally realised that common sense – the obvious answer – was in fact common non-sense. For almost 2,000 years, for instance, people believed Aristotle's commonsense assertion that unless things are continually pulled or pushed by some force they soon slow down naturally to rest. It took the brilliance of Galileo to fully realise that the role played by friction in slowing things down is crucial. Things don't have a natural tendency to slow down at all. The opposite is true; a moving object will keep moving at the same speed unless something slows it down, and that slowing force is usually friction. That idea is so ingrained now that this now seems common sense, too – but it wasn't until Galileo showed it.

With sailing boats, the commonsense answer isn't the right one, either, as I imagine anyone who has real experience of sailing will know. Sailboats now are actually very rarely driven by the wind pushing the sails from behind, despite what common sense tells you.

That wasn't true of the first sailboats. They were probably square rigs – that is, square sails hung from a beam or yard from the mast, across the boat at right angles. These were simple and effective. And these did catch the wind from behind the common sense way. The boat was always downwind, and 'ran' before the wind as the wind pushed against the sail. Because the wind was behind the boat, the boat would remain stable, despite the area of sail and the mast on top.

The wind didn't always have to be directly behind the boat. The yard could pivot up to 45° to catch the wind from different angles. And by tacking – that is, zig-zagging – these simple square-rigged boats could even make headway against a wind blowing from in front (though not closer to the wind direction than about 70°). But these simple square-riggers could never sail faster than the wind.

But then, around 2,000 years ago, somewhere in the Middle East probably, fore-and-aft sails were invented. This was a huge and often underappreciated technological breakthrough. Unlike the simple square rig, which stretches across the boat at right angles, the fore-and-aft sail is set up in line with the boat. Fore-and-aft sails can be square in shape, but the earliest were all triangular 'lateen' sails, still seen today in Arab dhows. The top edge of the triangle was hung from a yard mounted on the mast and slanting down at an angle from the aft of the boat. The bottom aft corner was left free and secured by ropes.

Lateen sails work in an entirely different way to square sails. With lateens, the sail acts like an aerofoil. In fact, they are driven by the wind blowing *across* the sails at an angle. When the sail is at the correct angle to the wind, the sail bows out and the sails create 'lift' like an aeroplane's wings because of the difference in air pressure either side of the sail created by the curve of the sails. Of course, the lift is horizontal, drawing the boat forward, not vertical as it is with an aeroplane.

The pressure on the sail tends to tip the boat over sideways, so a keel on the bottom of the boat is essential to reduce the chances of the boat capsizing – and also to ensure the boat maintains its angle to the wind and so keep the pressure on the sails up. It's the balance between the pressure of the wind and the lateral pressure of the water that keeps the boat skimming forward.

With a lateen sail, a boat can 'beat' much closer to the wind – that is, it can sail almost into the wind. Early lateen boats could sail just 40° from the wind direction at very best; some modern yachts can manage less than 20°. Typically, normal cruising yachts sail at about 45° off the apparent wind (the wind relative to the boat); modern performance racing yachts typically sail at about 27°. If the sails maintain the correct angle to the wind, they can create enough lift to draw the boat along faster than the wind. This is what some modern catamarans can do well.

The fastest catamarans can sail twice as fast as the wind, and some sand yachts can sail three times faster. In 2012, Paul Larsen's trimaran-cum-hydrofoil Vestas Sailrocket managed to smash the world sailing speed record by reaching 65.45 knots – two and a half times the wind speed! Larsen believes it can go faster still.

Why does a tennis ball spin? (Physics, Cambridge)

For a tennis fan, there are few sights more mesmerising than a perfect shot from Rafa Nadal on a clay court. The ball loops high and far over the net. As it comes down, it looks as if it's too long. The crowd sigh. Then, as if Nadal's got the ball on a string, or a magic force-field at his disposal, the ball suddenly drops, just on the baseline. It's in! What's more, as the ball spins off the clay in a brief puff of dust, it suddenly accelerates, so that Nadal's opponent mistimes his shot and shanks it way into the air. He's been the victim of Nadal's celebrated topspin. Nobody does it like Nadal on clay!

Roger Federer, one of the world's great players, puts an astonishing 2,700 revolutions per minute of spin on a ball on some of his forehand ground strokes. But that's nothing compared to Nadal, who can set the ball spinning at over 5,000 revolutions per minute.

Of course, a tennis ball doesn't spin all the time. Sometimes it can bounce flat off a player's racquet and fly straight and true over the net and perform exactly as Newton's laws of gravity say it should. It will loop down to the ground as soon as the acceleration due to gravity exceeds the acceleration imparted by the tennis ace's mighty thwack. And when it hits the court on the far side, it will bounce on towards the far end of the court, leaving the ground at pretty much the same (but opposite) angle that it landed.

So that's what happens on the actually quite rare occasions when the player hits the ball squarely. That is, the racquet is swung towards the ball in exactly the opposite direction that it arrives with the racquet face at right angles. If the player slices the racquet at an angle to the ball's flight, the racquet and ball will meet at an angle and then something different happens.

Effectively, the racquet is dragged over the ball when it impacts, and the friction between racquet and ball makes the ball roll briefly over the face of the racquet as it arrives. As it bounces back, it continues to roll or spin. The flatter and faster the racquet slices across the ball, the more the ball will spin – provided the main force of the racquet on the ball is still forward. To maximise the spin, the striker needs to whip the racquet over the ball at top speed at the same time as driving forward to send the ball over the net.

If the racquet is sliced over the top of the ball, the top of the ball spins forward and the bottom spins backwards. So the ball spins towards the opponent as it leaves the racquet. This is topspin. It requires a lot of energy because the top of the ball is typically already spinning towards the striker after bouncing off the court, so he is having to reverse its spin.

If the racquet is sliced under the ball, the top of the ball spins backwards and the top spins forwards.

So the ball spins back towards the striker as it leaves the racquet. This is backspin, and requires less energy because the striker is spinning it in the same direction it's already spinning.

As the spinning ball travels through the air, it interacts with it. Because the fluffy surface of a tennis ball is quite rough, the friction drags a thin layer of air around with the ball as it spins. So with a topspinning ball, the ball drags the air over and down at the front and under and the opposite way at the back, and creates a turbulent wake behind the top of the ball. As the ball's forward momentum drops and the ball begins to loop down, the drag and turbulence have more and more effect, making the ball drop suddenly, much earlier than gravity alone would make it.

Isaac Newton noticed this phenomenon as long ago as 1672, when watching his fellow students play tennis in Cambridge, but it is called the Magnus effect after the German physicist Gustav Magnus who studied it in the 1850s. The Magnus effect comes into play in many ball sports. Spinners in cricket use it to fool batsmen, as the ball suddenly drops earlier than they expect. Baseball pitchers use it to throw curveballs. It's surprisingly sensitive to air conditions and becomes much more pronounced when the air is humid. If the wind is blowing towards the striker, the effect will be even more exaggerated.

For the player trying to return a spinning ball, the

problems don't end with its tricky deviation in the air. As soon as it hits the ground, the spin makes it bounce in surprising ways. With topspin, the spin adds to the natural roll of the ball as soon as it bites the ground, and so it shoots off faster than it actually landed. With back-spin, the effect is the reverse, and the ball can almost stop dead in the air as it bounces. The extra friction on clay courts magnifies this effect; the slickness of grass, especially when damp, minimises it.

Federer on form is one of the best strikers of the ball tennis has ever seen, hitting it incredibly fast and true. But no wonder he prefers playing Nadal, the king of spin, on grass. On clay, Nadal is very, very difficult to beat. A spinning tennis ball has made Rafa the 'King of Clay', winner of the French Open an amazing eight times already at the time of writing.

Would Mussolini have been interested in archaeology? *(Archaeology, Oxford)*

Of course, few national leaders, if any, have ever taken such a public interest in archaeology as Benito Mussolini. Only Hitler and Stalin (tellingly) have shown quite the same archaeological zeal in the last century as 'Il Duce'. Mussolini ordered the excavation of many Roman ruins such as the Forum and the Colosseum, and it was he who authorised the massive project to entirely drain Lake Nemi and recover the two sunken Roman ships that had lain on its bed since the time of Caligula. But he didn't just authorise projects like these, he actively drove them forward, and frequently visited the sites to see what the diggers had unearthed.

Indeed, Mussolini made the most of any connection with Ancient Rome that he could. The symbol and very name of the Fascists came from the Ancient Roman *fasces*, bundles of birch rods used as an emblem of authority. And Mussolini liked to think of himself as a second Augustus.

One imagines the questioner would know all this, and know that it is one of the better-known facts about Mussolini – since as much as he was hailed for it in Italy, he was mocked abroad even at the time for his ostentatious concern for Ancient Rome. So the question must be hinting that there are doubts about the authenticity or sincerity of Mussolini's fascination for archaeology.

Of course, one cannot know Mussolini's mind, so the evidence must be purely circumstantial. And of course, I know I'm never going to be anything less than prejudiced when a leader as unsavoury as Mussolini is concerned. This is a man whose police indulged in torture and kidnapped children. A man who had many of his opponents put to death. A man who outlawed Jews. A man who ordered mass killings in Libya and Ethiopia. This is the brutal dictator of whom they said, condemning by their very omission, 'At least he made the trains run on time'.

It is hard to believe that anyone who was able to justify his crimes as a means to an end could ever have any genuine interest in anything that did not help his political agenda. One must believe that everything he did had an ulterior motive. And it seems highly likely that this was as true of his interest in archaeology as anything else.

It is surely no accident that Hitler and Mussolini, along with Albania's Enver Hoxha – brutal dictators all – seem to have had the same interest in archaeology. And the fact that it's a common interest is a strong sign that it's part of a pattern, rather than a personal interest. And, of course, it is.

Leaders have always been interested in the past, because it justifies their present and their future. If the past got you where you were, remind people of it. Ancestry gives rights of ownership, and always has done. But history became especially important in the 19th and 20th centuries as nation states began to define themselves and sought to firm up their identities. The German poet and thinker Johann Herder talked about the *Volkgeist*, the national character that emerges from history and homeland. History was a way of showing who you were and how you were different from other nations. The stronger your past, the stronger your identity. Throughout the 19th century, nationalism grew hand in hand with an interest in the past. In Britain at its imperial height, there was a renewed fascination in the legends of King Arthur and his Knights of the Round Table. The Scots were drawn in by tales of Rob Roy.

But under Hitler and Mussolini, this fascination with the past took a much more extreme and nasty turn. Hitler glorified the ancient past when Germany was pure and heroic and unsullied by other races. 'All great cultures of the past perished only because the originally creative race died out from blood poisoning,' he wrote. Mussolini's views were probably not so different, but for him it was the Roman Empire that was the heroic past of Italy – ironically the very Roman Empire whose defeat by German tribes led by Arminius in AD9 at Teutoburg was seen by the Germans as the defining moment in their past.

For Mussolini, the Roman Empire was the very symbol of the heights Italian culture could achieve and would again under him. Its propaganda value was immense, and he seized every opportunity he could to associate himself with it. Years of Fascist rule began to be identified in Roman numerals. The effete bourgeois handshake was replaced by the firm Roman salute. And once the Forum and Colosseum were properly excavated, he had a new road built to link them with the Fascist centre on Rome's Piazza Venezia. The drive behind this *romanita* (Roman-ness) was clearly not an interest in archaeology; it was image building. As Mussolini himself wrote at the time, 'My objective is simple; I want to make Italy great, respected and feared; I want to render my nation worthy of her noble and ancient traditions.' Roman heritage meant respect and fear for Italy, for the Fascists – nothing more.

There is no plainer evidence of Mussolini's disdain for genuine archaeology than the way it was done. Certainly there was a lot done in his time, more than at any time in the recent past, and Rome owes tourist attractions like the Forum to his Roman drive. But the sheer volume was part of the problem. It was shoddy archaeology, hurried and careless stripping away of the past by untrained, cheap labour. Small artefacts, the layers of valuable minutiae that tell archaeologists so much – everything was shovelled brutally aside in a bid to get at the more showy, but not necessarily more informative objects.

Moreover, Mussolini's real lack of interest for

archaeology was borne out by his complete disregard for anything of Rome's past (or even its living present) but relics of the Empire. Fascinating historic buildings from the medieval period and earlier, including homes and churches, were simply knocked away by his Empire-diggers, and the tenants who lived there shipped to Rome's outskirts, to get at the Roman treasure beneath.

In short, although we can never be absolutely certain, Mussolini's actions suggest he was only interested in archaeology as far as it boosted his image of himself, of the Fascists or of his version of Italy. Yes, he got archaeology done, but he wasn't interested in it – and at what price? The past was for Mussolini a place to plunder, not to explore.

Should poetry be difficult to understand? *(English Literature, Oxford)*

There's no doubt that poetry is often very, very hard to understand. Indeed this is often the biggest criticism held up by those with little interest in poetry. It's pretentious and elitist, they say – or just plain dull and meaningless complexity for the sake of it. If something's worth saying, they argue, it's better to say it plainly so everyone can appreciate it. It's not surprising that they react badly, of course, because all too often the obscurity of poetry makes people feel stupid and excluded – as if someone is rude enough to invite you to a dinner party then deliberately spend the evening speaking in a foreign language you don't understand.

Of course, there's a huge amount of poetry that's very easy to understand. Nursery rhymes are understandable to an infant, which is how it should be. Song lyrics are generally easy to understand, and often even facile, while many traditional songs have a straightforward poetic lyricism and narrative drive that directly inspired poets like Wordsworth and Coleridge (who many contemporaries thought obscure and difficult with their new style).

Simple poems written by poets can be profound and powerful works of literature, so it's certainly not that simple poems are inevitably lightweight and banal while difficult poems are heavyweight and sophisticated. Take Blake's poem 'London' for instance:

> I wander thro' each charter'd street,
> Near where the charter'd Thames does flow.
> And mark in every face I meet
> Marks of weakness, marks of woe.
>
> In every cry of every Man,
> In every Infants cry of fear,
> In every voice: in every ban,
> The mind-forg'd manacles I hear
>
> How the Chimney-sweepers cry
> Every blackning Church appalls,
> And the hapless Soldiers sigh
> Runs in blood down Palace walls
>
> But most thro' midnight streets I hear
> How the youthful Harlots curse
> Blasts the new-born Infants tear
> And blights with plagues the Marriage hearse.

Most people get this straight away, especially if read out loud, and similarly they get romantic poems like Elizabeth Barrett Browning's 'How Do I Love Thee?' (although there are some 'difficult' bits in this poem).

How do I love thee? Let me count the ways.
I love thee to the depth and breadth and height
My soul can reach, when feeling out of sight
For the ends of Being and ideal Grace.
I love thee to the level of every day's
Most quiet need, by sun and candlelight.
I love thee freely, as men strive for Right;
I love thee purely, as they turn from Praise.
I love with a passion put to use
In my old griefs, and with my childhood's faith.
I love thee with a love I seemed to lose
With my lost saints,—I love thee with the breath,
Smiles, tears, of all my life!—and, if God choose,
I shall but love thee better after death.

These are great poems. The expressive power, the rhythm of the language, the resonant imagery and the elevation of the emotion all make these among the best poems ever written. They do much, much more to stir the imagination and the intellect than mere doggerel. They are great poems because they leave a lasting and deep impression on the mind. They take you on a memorable journey that makes you feel you have learned something about life.

Blake's 'London' is so powerful and disturbing that it lingers with you as an unforgettable image of an unimaginably cruel city – indeed it is so telling that it makes us look at London anew today, not just London in Blake's time. Browning's description of her love is something we most of us recognise, or aspire to, in a love affair, but the imagery and choice of words elevate that love into something grander and more beautiful than we had maybe ever imagined before. Yet it touches deeply and resonates once Browning shows us this. Yes, that is how I do feel in love, that is how I might want to feel sometime. Oh to be in love like that – what an indescribable (by us) thrill!

These poems are great poems, yet they are on the whole easy to understand. So it is clear that poems don't have to be hard to be good. So if poems can be brilliant and profound yet not be inaccessible, why should they ever be difficult?

There is a problem, of course, in that much bad poetry does hide behind a veil of obscurity and complexity, as does much bad art and music. But that doesn't mean that all difficult poetry is pretentious display. The best, most lastingly memorable poetry strives to heighten our experience of life, to extend our ideas or our emotions. Sometimes that heightening might be done with simple language, but sometimes it can only be done with difficult language, difficult images and difficult ideas. As Robert Browning, the subject and object of Elizabeth Barrett Browning's poem, wrote: 'A man's reach should exceed his grasp,/Or what's a heaven for?'

Even the Blake and Barrett Browning poems I described as simple are 'difficult' compared to many pop lyrics, though. There is a reason for this. There is a great gulf between the best poetry and many popular song lyrics (and bad doggerel). Both are often made up from words and images in metre and rhyme, characteristics of poetry. But the ideas in these poems are not simplistic, even though the language and imagery is simple, and they last in the memory because of their depth of meaning, which goes beyond the simple first reading.

Sometimes, though, that important new experience or insight the poet is interested in can *only* be communicated with a difficult poem. That might be because the intellect or the emotions can only be triggered into the insight the poet wants to express by complex and involved language, imagery or concepts. Or it might be because the situation that the poet is writing about is difficult itself. Poetry can deal with death, the pain of love, and many other things that are difficult – and perhaps only explored fully through difficult poems.

As the American modernist poet Wallace Stevens wrote, 'poetry is a destructive force'.* It is not always destructive, of course, but it can be so in the broadest sense – it can shake you to the core, and

---

* It was the title of a poem in his 1942 collection *Parts of a World*.

upset you and be difficult to understand. It deals in uncomfortable, difficult areas of life. But that certainly doesn't mean such ideas for poetry should be avoided. Indeed, these are the ideas that many of the great poets are naturally drawn to, precisely because they are challenging.

Moreover, there is something exciting for the reader about being challenged, and then getting the thrill of understanding, or even partially understanding. Studying a difficult poem can be an immensely rewarding experience. If the poem gives a hint that there is something profound, something worth striving for beyond the difficult first impression, you may persist, work hard at understanding it fully and enrich your experience of the poem with each new insight. That's much easier to do with historic poems, because they've stood the test of time, so that many others testify that they are great poems and worth the effort; it's slightly harder with modern poets we are unsure will reward our labours.

Shakespeare is far from easy for us to read today, and we are assured it is worth making the effort to understand – and I know from my experience that this is true. The more effort I put into understanding every nuance of Shakespeare's verse, the more rewarding I find it. Indeed, I am disappointed when I hear actors speaking his verse and hearing they have not quite understood it fully enough. Interestingly, those actors who have understood it make it easier for us as audiences to understand, too.

Poetry was originally entirely oral, and it's interesting that the idea of spoken poetry is coming back into fashion. Rap poetry and slam poetry are opening up poetry to a whole new and young audience who might shun more traditionally written poetry. For the audience, this poetry has a high recognition factor, and immediately strikes a chord; they rarely find it difficult even though the rhythms can be complex and the subject matter challenging. But I often personally find this poetry hard to understand, not because it is intellectually convoluted, but because my ear is not sufficiently attuned to the rhythms, choice of words and accents to get what's being said. The whole stance of these poets – being sharp and streetwise, for instance – makes it clear that being hard to understand is not part of the purpose; it is just a side effect of the style for people like me.

That provides an interesting insight into 'difficult' conventional poetry – it may simply be a *lingua franca* one isn't familiar with. Here are some lines from Jeremy H. Prynne's poem* 'Streak~~~Willing~~~Entourage Artesian' (2009):

---

* There was a fascinating article in the *Los Angeles Review* in 2011 by Geoff Nicholson in which he describes his terrifying interview with Prynne for a place at Gonville and Caius College,

> Cornice buffed to distrained volume how much
> worn as cloud treading a skyline, dependency
> revoked a figure told up marking did you see
> run to it. For to run intrinsic the water gate ...

It's certainly not easy to get straight away! Fans of Prynne's work write that the image which used to stick to this poet of being somewhat pretentious and obscure is a misjudgement, and that he is actually one of the great poets of the last hundred years. I don't get his meaning yet myself, but there is plenty to intrigue and plenty to suggest that if I made the effort to learn the 'language' of Prynne's poems, I might be rewarded – and actually plenty to engage even if I don't understand much.

So, poetry doesn't have to be hard to understand but it often must be to deal with challenging subjects, or to challenge us. Whenever it slips into simply being easy to understand for the sake of it, it is in danger of slipping

---

Cambridge to read English Literature (http://lareviewofbooks.org/ essay/mentors-j-h-prynne#_) and what it was like being his student there. 'We heard that a previous intake of students had sat Prynne down and said, more or less, "All right Jeremy, what the fuck is this poetry of yours all about?" And he had explained himself splendidly: the skeptics were converted into ardent admirers. My crowd didn't force him to do that. Perhaps we simply didn't want to do what previous students had done, but in any case it didn't matter. Whether we "understood" Prynne's poetry or not, we were ardent admirers already. The obscurity was part of the appeal.'

into mediocrity. Simple poems can be great; but so too can the most difficult. Shakespeare, of course, has a wonderful way of describing the trickery of the poet that is both beautifully self-deprecating yet also exciting (though Theseus means it belittlingly):

The poet's eye, in a fine frenzy rolling,
Doth glance from heaven to Earth, from Earth to heaven;
And as imagination bodies forth
The forms of things unknown, the poet's pen
Turns them to shape, and gives to airy nothing
A local habitation and a name.
Such tricks hath strong imagination

—Theseus in Shakespeare's
A Midsummer Night's Dream

What is the square root of –1?

(Maths, Oxford)

This is perhaps the most elusive number in maths, still not entirely answered after millennia of trying by pretty much all the greatest mathematicians. The problem is not just with 1, but with any negative number. A square root must be the number which, when squared, gives the original number. So the square root of 9 is 3 (3 × 3 = 9), the square root of 4 is 2 (2 × 2 = 4) and the square root of 1 is 1 (1 × 1 = 1). But it doesn't work with negative numbers, because any two negatives multiplied together is positive, so –2 × –2 = (+)4, and –1 × –1 = (+)1.

So how can you find the square root of a negative number such as –1? The fact is you can't and so mathematicians call them 'imaginary' numbers. They might just as well have called them impossible numbers, or absurd numbers, or downright silly numbers, because they don't appear to exist. And yet we'd find it hard to live without them nowadays. They're vital for cutting-edge quantum science, but they're also vital in the design of aircraft wings and suspension bridges. They're imaginary because they cannot be tagged to any real number, yet they are 'real' because they are part of the real world. So they are paradoxically both imaginary and real, impossible yet possible.

This ambiguity was discovered by the Ancient

Egyptians long ago, and one of the great mathematicians of the ancient world, Hero of Alexandria, came across it nearly 2,000 years ago when he tried to calculate the volume of a pyramid sliced off across the top. In his calculations, Hero needed to find the square root of 81 − 144. The answer is, of course, √−63. This is negative so there is no calculable root, so Hero simply switched the sign to a plus and said the answer was √63. It was, of course, a complete fudge, but what else could Hero do? Even negative numbers were regarded warily in his time, so the idea of square roots of negatives was a complete no-no.

Medieval mathematicians came across the problem sometimes when they worked on cubic equations, but they simply dismissed negative roots as 'impossible' numbers. It was the (apparently) rather disreputable Italian astrologer Girolamo Cardano who finally began to break the deadlock, and perhaps it needed an outsider to ask the impossible. Cardano ended up as astrologer to the Vatican, but not before he began to explore the root of −1 in his book *Ars Magna* in 1545. He argued that such a number was possible, though he considered it utterly useless.

In his 1572 book *Algebra*, Rafael Bombelli was more positive about negatives. What Bombelli proved was that multiplying two of these imaginary numbers always gave a real number. He was doubtful himself at first about what he was saying, 'The whole matter seemed to rest on sophistry rather than truth,' he wrote. 'Yet I sought so long, until I actually proved this [real result] to be the case.'

Over the next two centuries, numerous mathematicians expressed their opinion, some accepting the idea of roots of negatives, others rejecting them out of hand. In the end, it was the genius of the then quite elderly Swiss mathematician Leonhard Euler (1707–1783) to resolve the dilemma. He introduced the 'imaginary unit', the symbol i. The symbol i is the imaginary number that when squared gives −1. So i can be written $\sqrt{-1}$. Euler's insight meant the square root of any negative number could be included in equations simply as i times the square root of the number. He went on to say that the roots of all negative numbers, $\sqrt{-1}$, $\sqrt{-2}$, $\sqrt{-3}$ and so on, are imaginary numbers, but 'imaginary' doesn't mean they are nonsense; it's simply a mathematical term for them.

The symbol i was a simple but brilliant solution, which allowed mathematicians to at last use $\sqrt{-1}$ and the square roots of other negative numbers in equations, with those other roots simply being expressed in terms of the unit i. It meant that mathematicians didn't need to address the ultimate nature of imaginary numbers; they could simply use them as a practical tool.

Yet the paradox remained. Exactly as Euler's invention of the symbol i and the concept of imaginary units made imaginary numbers a reality, so he also acknowledged they were impossible, writing, 'we may assert they are neither nothing, not greater than nothing, nor less than nothing, which necessarily renders them imaginary or impossible.' Although there were plenty of sceptics, that didn't bother Euler. If they work mathematically, he saw, imaginary numbers are as real as real numbers.

Euler's insight was to realise that we don't have to have all the answers to explore different areas. There may be a mystery at the heart of imaginary numbers, and the square root of −1, but it doesn't mean we cannot use it. With similar boldness, Newton had presented his theory of gravity purely as a mathematical construct without ever pretending to have any idea how such action-at-a-distance could ever work. We still don't know how gravity works, but Newton's theory remains one of the vital cornerstones of science. Similarly, imaginary units have proved hugely valuable in practical terms and are familiar to most advanced mathematicians today, even though they remain essentially a mystery. It's a proof that imagination and mathematical logic are not contradictions.

Imagine we had no records of the past at all, except everything to do with sport – how much of the past could we find out about? *(History, Oxford)*

I'm going to assume that this strange circumstance arose because all other records have mysteriously vanished, rather than that these were the only records that were ever made. If they turned out to be the only records ever made, it'd throw a very different light on our understanding of the past to discover our ancestors were so sports-obsessed.

Of course, real records about sport in the past beyond the last 150 years are quite scanty, since it was never something people thought to keep records about. Records were for more serious things, on the whole. So the answer to this question must be speculative – and based on the idea that we have much, much more extensive records about sport than we actually do. The question says 'everything to do with sport' but I guess we must limit this to things directly related, since including every record that was even just tenuously connected would cover just about every kind of record and would in some ways be more complete even than the records we already have.

Much of historical research is about building up a picture from very small clues. Historians of the ancient world can figure out trading patterns and international relationships, for instance, from the remnants of amphora (ancient wine storage jars) alone. So it is quite possible that the ingenuity of historians in working out what are useful clues and what are not could reveal a great deal about even the most distant past.

If, for instance, we had an entirely complete record of the identities of athletes competing in the ancient Olympic games, and also of the celebrities and dignitaries present, we could learn a great deal about shifting international relationships at the time. The catering might reveal a great deal about the diet of people at the time, while the origin of the foods involved might tell us about trading patterns.

Similarly, we might learn a great deal about the structure of Roman society from records of the building of the Colosseum and other sports arenas across the empire. We'd learn about Roman building technology. We'd learn the status of different tasks on the project and about the people involved, and their different roles might give us a good insight into the structure of Roman society. We'd learn which cities came to enough prominence to earn themselves a stadium, and about the economic state of different parts of the empire. We'd learn about the administration that commissioned it. We'd learn about Roman engineering practices and we'd learn about the movement of materials through the empire and how they were organised.

These might seem like scratching the surface of our

vast knowledge of these times. But if the records of sporting activities were truly complete, we would probably be able to piece together a great deal of this knowledge, about the racial and tribal origins and gender of both participants and spectators. Finding the dates of emperors, for instance, would be, I think, relatively easy, since emperors were patrons of many games, such as gladiator combats and chariot races. And the shifts of locations of events might give us a good indication of the ebb and flow of the empire. The fact that such bloodthirsty sports as gladiatorial combats, throwing Christians to the lions and so on were popular tells us things about Roman society, too.

If we move forward to the Middle Ages, hunting records would reveal a great deal about the royalty and aristocracy of Europe. Hunting was very much the privilege of the elite. From the list of names of each hunting party alone, we'd learn pretty much all the kings (and some queens) and princes, and the make-up of their retinue, since most of their court would be obliged to join them on hunts. We'd learn where they were at different times, and learn when the hunts had to be suspended as wars went on.

Over in Mesoamerica, the Aztec ball game would reveal a great deal about Aztec society. The ball game or *ullamaliztli* may have first started as long ago as the time of the Olmecs, and was not just entertainment, but a political and religious event, too. Whenever the Aztecs

built a new settlement, the first thing they would do
was to create a shrine to the god Huitzilopochtli. The
very next thing they'd do was to erect a ball game court
beside the shrine. In Tenochtitlan, the palace and temple
were then built around the ball game court. Since the
game played such a key role in the social, political and
religious life of the Aztecs, and earlier Mesoamerican
civilizations, it is certain that full records of the games
would tell us a great deal about these civilizations.

These are just a few examples of how the more
prominent official sports might tell us about history.
But if the records are complete, they will tell us about
the unofficial sports too. Because there is no record
now, we have very little knowledge at all of sports
among the ordinary people. Yet there is every chance
that they played sport. It seems highly unlikely that
ordinary people only became sports fans and participants in the late 19th century when records began to
be made. Indeed, we know that the second English
Civil War actually began on 22 December 1647 when
Roundhead armies tried to break up a local street football game between local townspeople in Canterbury.

So sports were clearly played by ordinary people, but
at the moment we only get fleeting snapshots of them.
The mine of information we'd have at our disposal if
we had complete records of village football matches,
local archery contests and all the unknown, as yet
unrecorded sports people played would be very rich.

We'd learn about the way the famous English arch-ers trained for the battle of Agincourt, for instance, with archery competitions in Islington near London – just who these archers were and from which walks of English (and as it happens Welsh) society. These archery competitions are among the few actually known and recorded. But surely there were many, many more unrecorded.

Maybe we'd even learn about things such as when writing began in different parts of the world from the dates of the earliest sports records. Wouldn't it be fantastic to read the first cuneiform match reports of the cup final in the Sumerian city of Eridu some 6,000 years ago? Maybe we'd learn about the develop-ment of paper, or printing, and much more.

Indeed, the possibilities of what we could learn about the past from complete sporting records would excite any historian. We wouldn't find out about many things we know and take for granted now. We'd cer-tainly lose the myriad personal stories and details that make the study of history so rich and engaging. But we'd learn at least some of the bigger picture, and we'd learn about many, many things we just have no knowledge or certainty of now. So let's hope one day the Ancient Chinese *Wisden* and the Viking Looting League archives and many other sports records actu-ally turn up. Come on, you Odinsboys …

How do you see through glass? *(Physics, Cambridge)*

If you are of a biblical turn of mind, you might answer 'darkly,' finishing off the famous passage from Paul's letter to the Corinthians in which he explains that our view of the divine is somewhat indistinct. Yet a scientific answer to this question is actually every bit as opaque as the theological.

It seems a simple, familiar phenomenon, and on one level, it is. Glass is transparent and lets light rays pass straight through; other solid substances are opaque and block the passage of light. But when you think about it a little more, it becomes more perplexing. When you see through glass, you are seeing the pattern of light beyond the glass transmitted unaltered, as if there was nothing at all in between. Yet glass is a solid. So how is it that light can pass through glass and not other solid substances?

One answer lies in the realm of advanced quantum physics or, to be precise, that devilish realm of quantum physics known as quantum electrodynamics, or QED. QED is the science that describes how light and matter interact, pioneered by Richard Feynman half a century ago.

The crucial thing to remember in QED is that light can sometimes be thought of as streams of unimaginably tiny massless particles called photons, as Einstein first realised. So when light comes towards a window pane – or any other solid surface – you have to think about lots of tiny photons entering a field of atoms, like a horde of fleeing rebel soldiers hurtling into a forest.

Somewhere near the heart of every atom is a nucleus. In relation to the atom, the nucleus is, as the famous physicist Ernest Rutherford so memorably described it, about the size of a gnat in the Albert Hall. So the chances of the hurtling photons actually encountering a nucleus are pretty remote!

But surrounding the nucleus is a whirling fog of tiny electrically charged particles known as electrons. If you think of electrons and photons as like billiard balls, they'd be so ridiculously tiny that the chances of any photons encountering electrons are even less than their chances of interacting with the nucleus – about as slim as the only two gnats in London accidentally colliding – and bricks would be as transparent as glass. But photons are actually electromagnetic energy, just like electrons, and as they get even remotely near atoms, their electric fields interact.

When light strikes matter, the photons rarely go straight through. Instead, they may be drawn in by electrons – as if, in our woody analogy, our fleeing soldiers were caught up in the undergrowth between the trees – and the electrons soak up their energy. In opaque substances, much of this energy turns into heat, which is why walls heat up in the sun. In window glass, however, many of the electrons stay only briefly energised or 'excited' before letting the extra energy go as a new photon, usually with identical energy.

So when light shines through a window, the photons don't go straight through at all. Instead, they get absorbed by the atoms in the glass – and then re-emitted several times before they finally emerge the other side. And it's only highly probable they'll emerge, not certain.

But why is that the electrons absorb the photons in most solids, but transmit them in glass? It's all to do with energy levels. Electrons sit at particular energy levels as they buzz around the nucleus, but if they absorb a photon they are bounced up to a higher level. In opaque solids, photons probably have enough energy to propel electrons up to higher levels. But glass is a special kind of solid, known as an amorphous solid, and it seems that in such solids the gaps between energy levels are much wider – and the energy needed to power the jump is probably beyond that of photons of visible light, which is why many are not absorbed. So visible light is mostly slowed down by glass; a much smaller proportion is scattered, reflected or absorbed. But there *is* enough energy in photons of ultraviolet light, which is why UV is absorbed by glass.

On the whole, the re-emission of photons happens so quickly that the transmission of light through glass, although slowed to half the speed of light in a vacuum, is all but instantaneous. But science fiction writers have talked, perhaps fancifully, about 'slow glass'. This could be a window through which light travels so slowly that you could pack it up, take it round the world, and then see the view outside months later. In 2013, researchers from France and China embedded dye molecules in a liquid crystal matrix to slow the group velocity of light down to less than one billionth of its top speed. (With sodium atoms chilled to within a millionth of a degree of absolute zero, in a state called a Bose-Einstein condensate, light can be brought to a complete standstill.) In 2013, too, intriguingly, scientists at the University of Southampton used a laser to rearrange the atoms in the crystals of glass, to create a phenomenal 'crystal memory'. Three hundred and sixty terabytes of data could be stored in a piece of glass no bigger than a CD with such stability that it would last for centuries.

One of the most extraordinary features of glass, though, is not its transparency but partial reflections. The explanations at a quantum level are so hard to fathom that I won't even attempt one here.

I've chosen to try an admittedly fuzzy quantum explanation of the transparency of glass in responding to the question 'How do you see through glass?' but of course there are other avenues that might be explored. One could focus, for instance, on the 'How do you see' part of the question and look at the science of human vision, for instance – not just the physical reception of images through the eyes, but the whole remarkable process of registering these images in the brain. That might seem simpler ...

Can a thermostat think? *(Experimental Psychology, Oxford)*

If you were to say thinking is just something brains do, then the simple answer must be 'no', since a thermostat does not possess a brain. But what is thinking? Is it possible to think without a brain?

Thinking is something we do every day and every night. Our lives are filled with thoughts. Some are trivial. Some profound. Some funny. Some sad. Some clever. Many more not so clever ... Thoughts whirl through our heads non-stop – even more so when we deliberately try to stop thinking.

Sometimes we are conscious of our thoughts. Sometimes they bubble away in the back of our minds without us being aware of them. Try thinking about thinking and you suddenly become aware that your head is spinning with thoughts – but you can only catch a few of them as they flash by. So thinking is connected to consciousness but is not the same thing, and a thermostat would not necessarily need to be conscious to be capable of thinking. (I'll come back to this later.)

In the past, when they thought about thoughts, thinkers used to think that thought is not connected with the physical world at all. Thought is something the mind does, but it is not material; it is the 'soul' or some other immaterial quality that simply uses the body as a conduit. When Descartes famously used thinking as the one irreducible proof of his existence, 'I think, therefore I am', he was not talking about any physical process; the mind was for him like the audience watching physical reality played out as if on a stage. The mind had no physical location. Thought was seen as a very special and unique faculty of humankind – indeed the main quality that makes us human.

Nowadays, though, most experimental psychologists would assert that thinking is entirely a material activity, and that it goes on in the brain. The mind and brain are the same thing. Philosophically, of course, this reflects the rise of science, but there are a number of clues that this must be so. First of all, our thoughts seem intimately connected with the state of our brains. Have one or two shots of malt whisky too many, for instance, and your thoughts get scrambled. Another clue is in the fact that we evolved from purely physical organisms – so it seems less likely that we suddenly developed an immaterial mind.

What's more, modern fMRI scanners have now been able to watch the brain in action and actually see it thinking. Amazingly, in spring 2014, a team of researchers at Yale used scanners to pick up the pattern of activity in the brains of six subjects in such detail that they were able to reconstruct and identify faces the subjects were looking at.

So thinking is a physical activity of the brain, and although the human brain takes thinking to a different level, even the tiniest creature with the tiniest brain might therefore be capable of thinking in some way. Not every scientist would wholly concur with this reductionist view, but since we're interested here in a purely physical mechanism, the thermostat, it makes sense to stick with it for now.

Brains are, of course, little more than bundles of nerve cells, which by themselves are simply mechanisms for passing on signals. That in itself is not thinking. Physiologists talk about reflex arcs, when they talk about the way your hand pulls away instantly on touching something hot. The 'hot' nerve signal from the hand only travels as far as the spinal cord before short-circuiting back to the hand muscles to jerk them away. The pain only registers in the brain later, and thank goodness because by the time you thought about it and your brain told your hand to move it might be badly burned. And we talk about similar knee-jerk reactions and acting without thinking.

In some ways, a simple thermostat is very similar to a reflex arc. It's an automatic – and unthinking – response to a stimulus. Whenever your central heating gets too hot, the thermostat automatically switches it off as the sensors respond to the rise in temperature. And yet this is no more or less than what nerve cells do, and if brains are simply assemblies of nerve cells, is there necessarily any fundamentally different quality which a sophisticated thermostat could not have? Is a brain simply a mechanism that responds to stimuli and initiates a particular response, just like a thermostat? Computers demonstrate just how sophisticated and intricate a stimulus-and-response mechanism can be, given a sufficiently clever processing network.

Perhaps it's worth looking at the difference between a reflex and thought – or even between the reception in the brain of a perception, such as what you see and hear and smell before you, and a thought. The perception may be rich in detail. There may even be a recognition of patterns, such as running, or even concepts, such as 'dangerous lion'. But ultimately it's just recording. Intuitively, we know there is a difference between this and thinking, but it's not so easy to pin down just what this is.

One way of looking at thinking is that it's about making connections. Most animals can *perceive* an apple falling – and many machines can record or respond to such an event if they have the right sensors – but you have to *think* to appreciate that the seeds it contains are the beginnings of a new tree. And you have to think like Newton to make the connection between the falling apple and the movement of the planets and come up with a theory of gravity. That ability to spot hitherto unknown connections seems to be central to the process of thinking, and it seems way beyond any thermostat. It may be beyond many simple animals, too, and may be the distinguishing feature between complex, thinking animals like us, and simple creatures that live by instinct alone.

Some house central heating thermostats are now termed 'smart', because they respond to your behaviour to keep the house warm on the minimum of energy, shutting off when you go out and close the door, for instance, then switching on again half an hour before your usual time home so that you walk into a toasty warm house. Connections seem to be being made here, albeit simple ones, so perhaps the smart thermostat *is* thinking. Intuitively, it would seem not; it does seem to be just a slightly more sophisticated reflex. So perhaps our definition of thought as making connections is not adequate. The limitations of the smart thermostat's response is that the connections are programmed into its processor when it is built.

Thinking seems to be about creating *new* connections, and that's something that even a smart thermostat can't do. Could it do so if it were controlled, in the future, by a sophisticated computer that completely controlled your environment, making adjustments to whatever new conditions came along?

We're entering a more grey area, here, or perhaps a more grey matter area. But still, I would say no, it is not thinking, for two reasons: first because its range of options in terms of its inputs and outputs is still limited; and secondly because we come back to the question of consciousness.

It is certainly possible to argue that the range of inputs and outputs to thinking brains is limited, too, and that it's only a question of degree. But that degree seems significant. The difference between a worm and a human is only a question of degree – they are both biological mechanisms made from the same organic materials with many similar basic structures – but the degree really matters.

Secondly, although it is true that thoughts whirl through our head without our being conscious of them, without that consciousness, those thoughts are simply white noise. It takes consciousness to register those thoughts, pick them out and give them meaning. So consciousness does seem to be crucial to thinking, after all. Ideas of consciousness are complex, and understanding it has remained one of the most elusive goals of science. All the same, by any definition it seems unlikely that any thermostat could ever be considered conscious. So on this basis alone I would say a thermostat cannot think. Of course, when a thermostat gets offered a place at Oxbridge ahead of a human candidate, I might have to think again …

Why might erosion make mountain ranges higher? (Geography, Cambridge)

On every continent, mountains tower above us some-where, vast, solid expressions of the Earth's geological power. 'As old as the hills', the expression goes, yet the world's biggest mountain ranges are all quite young in geological terms. The rugged ridges of the Rockies, the snowy summits of the Alps, the majestic heights of the Himalayas have all risen from the plains within the last 50 million years. That means the dinosaurs died out long before they ever got a chance to scale even the foothills.

There would have been other great mountain ranges for the flying dinosaurs to soar over, though, moun-tains now long much reduced by the power of ero-sion, such as the Scottish Caledonians, the American Appalachians and the Asian Urals, perhaps the world's oldest mountains. However solid and immoveable they seem, mountain ranges are not permanent features of the Earth's surface. They are continually being raised up and brought low in endless sequences of geological upheaval and long exposure to the wind and rain.

In the 19th century, geologists came to believe that mountain belts are raised up in periods they called 'orogens' that lasted tens of millions of years or so, then stopped. And when these mountain-building phases cease, the rocks, newly exposed to the elements – wind, rain, frost, running water, moving ice – can be worn back down to sea level in only a little more time. In 1899, one of the great pioneers of geology, William Morris Davis, developed the idea of cycles of erosion, in which mountain ranges were raised up, worn down, then uplifted for the cycle to begin again. It seemed so beautifully simple that it was widely accepted.

But since the 1960s, a rather different picture has emerged. First of all, the discovery of plate tectonics has shown how mountain ranges are actually raised up. Plate tectonics show that the Earth's surface is far from being fixed. Instead it is made from 40–50 vast, continent-size slabs of rock – the tectonic plates – that continually shift this way and that, form and reform.

The world's longest range is actually the mid-ocean ridge that rises up where plates are moving apart under the sea, allowing new material to well up from the Earth's interior. But all the high ranges on land occur where plates are moving together, crumpling up the rocks in between like a rug pushed against a wall.

It's the plates beneath the oceans that do the most moving, and these 'fold' mountains are mostly thrown up along the edges of continents, where the ocean plate crunches against the continental plate. The ocean plate is dense compared to the buoyant continental rocks which float like rafts on the semi-molten interior of the Earth, so as it drives against the continent, the ocean plate gets thrust underneath, back into the Earth's interior.

As it does, a wedge of debris called a 'terrane' piles up between the opposing plates – and as the plates go on pushing together, these terranes are piled higher and higher in mountain belts like the American Rockies. Eventually, the ocean plate may vanish entirely into the interior leaving two continents to crunch together head-on, and throwing up the biggest ranges of all. That happened with the Appalachians and the Caledonians, and is now happening with the Himalayas as India ploughs relentlessly north into Asia.

In recent years, though, geologists have begun to realise that this is only half the story. For a start, over geological time, rocks are not rigid and brittle. Instead, they slowly flow. So the Himalayas are more like a giant bow wave in front of India than a rumpled carpet or a fractured rubble heap of rock.

Indeed, the whole picture of continents banging together and crumpling rocks up between them is looking rather too simplistic. When British scientist George Airy was surveying the Himalayas in the 19th century, he was surprised to find his plumb line deviating from the perpendicular, revealing that the mass of the mountains extends in deep roots far below the surface. We now know this is true of all great mountain ranges. In fact, mountains are like icebergs floating on the Earth's interior.

As mountains get worn away by the weather and other forces of erosion, they float up, like a raft losing some of its load, in a process called isostasy. So the ancient Appalachians, mountains geologists once thought were doomed to dwindling away for ever and ever, are actually getting higher by a few centimetres every century. Even though they are far from any mountain-building continental collisions, erosion has lightened the burden of rock and is allowing the Appalachians to rise jauntily above the plains.

Of course, erosion doesn't just begin the moment mountain-building begins; it's there right from the start. And the whole process is complicated by the effect of these geological shifts on climate and the forces of erosion. The uprise of the Himalayas, for instance, created a barrier to the steady flow of air over Asia, and kick-started the to and fro of monsoons that bless India with its alternating seasons of drought and torrential rain. The heavy monsoon rains intensify erosion, and wear away Himalayan rock so that, like the Appalachians, they drift on upwards isostatically.

This, combined with the crunch of folding rocks, make the Himalayas the world's fastest growing mountains, rising at over a centimetre a year. That might not sound so much, but it would add a kilometre in just a hundred thousand years. But the Himalayas' ascent may be slowing down, even as erosion is lightening the burden, because the Eurasian plate is stretching out and subsiding rather than only thrusting up as India drives on.

It's clear that the whole business of mountain-making is very far from a simple cycle of building up then laying low. Indeed, it's a complex and dynamic process involving a host of interacting factors, and erosion allows mountains to rise higher by lightening the burden of rock – but that's far from the end of the story. However it ends, though, the mountains will be with us for a long time.

Should a Walmart store be opened in the middle of Oxford? *(Economics and Management, Oxford)*

Walmart is not just a giant; it is a supergiant. It is the world's largest business, beating even Shell and Exxon in the Fortune 500 in 2014, with revenues of nearly half a trillion dollars. It employs more than 2 million people around the world and many more in companies that supply it. Even companies like General Motors and Nissan are fairly small by comparison.

What's astonishing is that it has been going barely 50 years. Walmart's super-powered growth has been down to one simple strategy – bringing its customers goods at the lowest possible price. The strategy has been extraordinarily successful. Walmart can sell goods cheaper than all but its largest rivals. It succeeds by undercutting other shops and putting them out of business to increase its market share. As it grows, its dominance delivers to Walmart huge power over suppliers, pushing down the price it pays to them. That, combined with economies of scale, keeps store prices to customers very low.

Walmart has come in for a lot of criticism in recent years, highlighted in the book *The Wal-Mart Effect* by Charles Fishman. Some of the effects Fishman identified are specific to Walmart, but most are just part of the increasing dominance of a handful of giant supermarket chains such as Tesco, as well as Walmart.

Critics like Fishman argued that big-box supermarkets like Walmart, usually located in out-of-town sites only reachable by car, have had a devastating effect on local economies and communities – tugging shoppers away from town centres to leave them as ghost towns, pushing down local wages and forcing independents out of business by undercutting. Their monopoly power often meant they were able to ride roughshod over local planning demands to set up business where they wanted, and drive business and development to them, regardless of local community needs.

Others, like Andrew Simms in his book *Tescopoly*, pointed out the wider impact of the supermarket spree on the world. To achieve uniformity, bulk deals and full stores at all times, the supermarket chains bring in food and other products over massive distances, dramatically boosting environmentally damaging 'food miles' and wasteful packaging. Their need for uniformity means that farmers are often forced to throw away up to half of their crop which doesn't fit the bill. Their demand for low prices from suppliers encourages factory farming techniques and poor animal welfare. Worse still, it can push the wages of farm workers both at home and in third-world countries to rock bottom.

The problems weren't exclusive to supermarkets but part of the growing concentration of retail power into the hands of just a few chains, who were able to under-cut independents with their economies of scale. People began to talk about 'Clone Towns', as just a small number of global chains appeared over and over again in cities around the world, so that every shopping centre from Shanghai to Sheffield had pretty much the same shops. The process seems to have been accelerated by the growth of online marketing, which makes it harder and harder for independent shops to survive.

As planners began to worry about the death of town centres, they began to be more wary about granting permission, and so there has been a drive by supermarket chains to move back into town centres with 'convenience' stores. Since Asda Walmart already has two big box stores on the outskirts of Oxford, one imagines the proposed city-centre store in the question is one of these convenience stores, since there isn't space for anything larger.

Oxford is an unusual city, in some respects, in that the university gives it a high resident population living right in the centre who have no car to get to big out-of-town supermarkets. Many of these often impoverished students may welcome the chance to buy a wide range of goods at the low prices a new city-centre Asda Walmart outlet might offer, especially if they are open long hours.

But is there a price to pay for this convenience? A chain like Asda Walmart with its global buying power will almost certainly ruthlessly undercut local competitors to build up its business. Tesco, when it has opened businesses, for instance, has offered 40 per cent discounts to local residents to get them through the doors. The low prices are good for residents in the short term, but if local independents are put of business as a result, it could dramatically reduce the diversity of city-centre retailing already hit by the global downturn and the growth of online sales. And research has shown that if a new supermarket is located just a short distance from the centre but not in it, it draws people away, and reduces footfall past other shops which are not even directly competing.

Vacancies in city-centre shops are rising, and the long-term effect of too many shops like Walmart may be to help kill the vibrancy of the city centre, and turn it into just a dead university campus, haunted entirely by dispirited academics who have no choice but to buy from the chains or online. There's a powerful argument, though, that this is just part of a realignment of city centres away from retailing into places of leisure as ailing shops are replaced by restaurants, bars and theatres, and this is simply the 'creative destruction' of the free market.

There is a high chance that if Walmart did plan to open a shop in Oxford centre, there would be a lot of local objection, just as there has been to the opening of similar stores in many towns across the UK. Many people are beginning to resent the power of global capitalism the big chains present, and don't want them in their neighbourhoods. They don't want the diversity of their local shops lost to clone towns. They don't want the undermining of the local economy these chains represent as they source their products from far away and push down wages. They disapprove ethically of the chains' effect on farming practices, and wages and conditions in developing countries. They are worried about the effect on the global environment these big businesses have, and much more. And I would be entirely with them.

There are other more practical problems. The 'just-in-time' stocking policy means extra trucks are drawn into streets not able to cope with them, and the noise of unloading can go on through the night, disrupting the sleep of city-centre residents.

In the town of Totnes, recently, local people campaigned to stop the Costa Coffee shop opening a branch in the town. I have a feeling Oxfordians would likewise campaign to block Walmart opening in Oxford.

Critics of these campaigners often argue that these campaigners have their heads in the sand, trying to fly in the face of market forces, or that they are a vocal minority who just don't want these things spoiling their neighbourhood while denying the chance of cheaper goods to those less well off than themselves. Chains like Asda Walmart, they insist, are only successful because enough people shop at them, appreciating the low prices and range of goods they can offer. Moreover, the opening of a store can, it is argued, create local jobs, bring shoppers into the area and so boost the local economy.

Even the most heritage-minded of local planners know they cannot pickle town centres in aspic, ruling against changes of use and development. If city centres are to stay thriving they must be lively and interesting enough, and offer enough of what people want, for people to be drawn in, and spend time and money to bring the area an income. So there is a balance to be struck between protecting what is good and allowing the freedom for change. This, though, is a balance which I think has slipped too far in favour of unfettered development and placed too much power in the hands of a handful of global corporations like Walmart, who have used their monopoly status to operate largely free of restraint. Maybe it's time the balance was tipped back in favour of community rather than market choice.

Is the moon made of green cheese?

(Veterinary Sciences, Cambridge)

It's just possible that space is just one giant cornucopia of dairy products, with a cheesy moon and the Milky Way mixing in with the yet-to-be-discovered Clotted Cream Nebula and Galactic Butter Churn. But I think it's unlikely, and I'd be worried about the size of the astronomical cow responsible for these lactarian colossi.

The idea that the moon is green cheese is one of those silly nonsenses that persist because its absurdity catches the imagination, just like the idea of boats sailing off the end of a flat Earth. No one ever really believed it, but it bears just enough resemblance to reality to appeal. The pits on the moon do make it look just a little like a big round cheese up there in the sky, though of course it's clearly not green, so maybe someone really said it was 'cream cheese', not green.

We know it's definitely not cheese now, green or cream, Camembert or Gorgonzola, because astronauts have been to the moon and brought back samples – and they're quite definitely rock. But we knew it wasn't cheese long before the Apollo missions.

Of course, we could never be certain when a distant view was all we had of the moon, but our knowledge of anything is based on inferences from things we can be certain of. Before the Middle Ages, no one really had any idea what the moon was made of. It floated in the sky, so it seemed likely that it was made of some very light material. But it looked like a sphere, and it seemed natural to speculate that it was a rocky sphere like the Earth.

With the invention of the telescope, astronomers could see features that looked like mountains and cliffs on the moon's surface – and they became increasingly certain that it is indeed a rocky sphere, with a landscape on a great scale like the Earth's. By the 19th century, using trigonometry on the shadows of the cliffs enabled astronomers to confirm that the cliffs on the moon were indeed on a similar scale to rock cliffs on Earth. What's more, the closer astronomers looked, the more they saw features that looked like volcanoes on Earth, and then features that looked like meteorite impact craters. Of course, no one could be absolutely sure, but science and knowledge moves forward by looking for correspondences with things we do know, testing our hypothesis whenever possible – and the correspondences between the Earth and moon seemed so strong that no one has doubted the moon is a rocky globe for a long time.

Of course, the Apollo astronauts might be lying, and really brought back a giant stash of dairy products which they're secretly leaking on to the market – or of course never went there at all, as some conspiracy theorists suggest. But I think frankly it's unlikely.

Philosophers have always had a problem with how

we know things. Rationalist philosophers insist that reason and deduction are the only reliable guides to knowledge, and that the senses can be misleading. Descartes famously asserted, of course, that there is nothing, logically, we can be certain of but the fact that we are thinking – 'I think, therefore I am' – and so the mind must be the starting point of any search for knowledge. Empiricists, on the other hand, assert that knowledge starts with the senses and can only be acquired through experience, and so distrust any ideas that cannot be verified by the senses.

In practice, we end up using a mixture of both on a day-to-day basis. It's that kind of mix that I have used above in explaining how people decided the moon wasn't green cheese. It's not so far from the process Plato described long ago as 'justified true belief'. Plato argued that there are three elements involved in my knowing something. First, that the fact is actually true; second, that I believe it to be true; and third, that I am justified in believing it to be true. So if the truth really is that the moon is not green cheese, then if I assert that it is not green cheese and I'm justified in that belief, then it's fair to say that I know it is not green cheese.

So the justification is crucial. Justification usually comes from three sources: empirical evidence (the evidence of the senses), authoritative testimony and logical deduction. In the moon's case, the justification comes from the overwhelming weight of evidence demonstrating its lack of cheesy qualities, and the near-certainty that every method I could conceive of proving it cheesy will fail. But I have not seen this evidence for myself, nor did I deduce it, so I am relying entirely on authoritative testimony.

The great Austrian-British science theorist Karl Popper (1902–1994), however, argued that justification isn't enough; a claim can only be accepted as knowledge if it is possible to show it could be false. So, although by Plato's book, I can say I know the moon is not cheesy from the weight of authoritative testimony that shows that it is not, by Popper's, I can merely say that I know of no evidence that it is.

Astronomers can very rarely actually visit the objects of their study, so they have to work out what they can mostly from observation and inference alone, and by looking for correspondences with things on Earth. Yet it is remarkable just how much this can reveal. Back in the 1830s, the French philosopher Auguste Comte said we could never possibly know what the stars were made of – they were just too far distant. Yet within just a few decades he was shown to be wrong, when William Huggins analysed the spectrum of colours in light coming from some stars and showed that they must be made mostly of hydrogen and helium. From spectroscopic analysis of light reaching the Earth from objects in space, astronomers can work out what pretty much every glowing object in space is made of – and they can work out what planets in the solar system are made of from the way they move through space, which demonstrates their mass and density. They may just be wrong, of course, but the correspondences means that their assumptions are unlikely to be untrue.

Increasingly, space missions have been able to visit the moon, Venus, Mars and other planets – and since everything confirms that our general interpretation of what they are made of is essentially sound, it reinforces our confidence in our assumptions. But maybe when the moon rock samples from the Apollo missions start to pong, or smell as if they could go well with a cream cracker and pickles, we may have to revise our theories.

What makes a strong woman? *(Theology, Oxford)*

Everyone has their own idea of what a strong woman is. For *Forbes* business magazine, which publishes an annual list of 'the world's most powerful women', it's top politicians and CEOs, activist billionaires and celebrities who 'matter,' like German chancellor Angela Merkel, Spanx CEO Sara Blakely and model Gisele Bündchen. For many pop followers, strong women are stars like Lady Gaga and Lorde who seem to take control of their own image. For community activists, it's those mothers who hold the family together. For religious believers, a strong woman is one whose faith and purity endures against the odds. For movie moguls, it's often feisty, sharp-witted girls who cut it with the lads, or wield a mean gun, or get their man before he gets them.

All these women have their own strengths. But asking the question about 'strong' women has encapsulated a problem. If you talked about a strong man, you'd be talking about a circus entertainer, maybe, or a brutal, unsophisticated leader. A strong *man* is a freak, a dunderhead, a thug, mostly. So why would we talk about a strong woman as if that's a good thing? In a way, it's just another way of saying it's a woman's fault if she is not treated with respect. If only she'd been stronger, then she could have overcome all the obstacles placed in her path!

Around the world today, countless women and girls are denied basic human needs. Countless woman and girls are subjected to difficult living conditions, abuse, child labour, sex trafficking, early and forced marriages, lack of education and income opportunity and other offences because they are born into cultures in which they are poorly valued. And millions of girls even in more enlightened cultures face continual problems with finding their place in the world, in being properly treated and valued in the workplace, in achieving the equality of status which should be their right as human beings.

By asking about 'strong women' as the question does, it's echoing that continual praise and focus on strong women, which implies that strong women are the shining examples, fighters who stand up for their gender. Stoical wives taming the prairies, kick-ass princesses with martial arts skills, femmes fatales outgunning any man with their cutting put-downs ... All of these are figures of admiration. But they are the odd-girls, the rare exceptions who seem to prove the rule – that if women are undervalued, it's their own fault because they're just too weak. *Forbes* identifies the women who matter. And so don't the other billions of women matter, then?

There are few more appalling examples of how misplaced this image of the strong woman can be than in a story I saw portrayed recently on stage in London.

The story is of the Birangona of Bangladesh. The
Birangona are the hundreds of thousands of women
and girls who were systematically raped, tortured and
abused during Bangladesh's war of independence. The
original crimes against them were indeed horrific, but
what is tragic, too, is the way they have been marginalised ever since. The word 'Birangona' means 'brave
women' – and yes, many have indeed been brave, and
the film footage in the stage production of some of
them moved you almost to tears with their courage. But
bravery seems entirely beside the point, when the real
and physical abuse of the war has been followed by four
decades of vilification in an independent Bangladesh
because they are 'fallen women'. No amount of bravery, no amount of 'strength' makes up for the abuse of
their situation. Why should they need to be brave, after
all they've been through? And what of those women
who are not 'brave', who are not so strong, those like
the Birangona woman on the film who longed for death
to end her humiliation?

The idea of the strong woman, in some ways, weak-
ens women. It's often condescending in the mouths of
men, like the sleazebag who says, 'I love strong women.'
It's often denial in the case of women who claim they
are strong. Like embracing Jean-Paul Sartre's image
of the person who denies who she is, and so cannot
change. Or like the man who announces to the world
that he's so cool – and immediately shows he isn't.

Pop culture seems to love songs about strong girls who kick metaphorical sand in the face of the man who treated them bad. But for many girls listening and trying to identify, it's a quick high before feeling even worse because they aren't sand-kickers themselves. Constantly praising strong women, however good the intention, only serves to remind women of what fragile flowers they really seem to be. They'll only be genuinely strong when no one needs to praise their strength.

Of course, this question was posed for theology, and the attitude of religions to women has been much under scrutiny in recent decades, with issues over everything from the wearing of the veil for Islamic women to the controversy over whether women should be allowed to be bishops in the Church of England.

Some conservative Christians are deeply opposed to women being given any strength or authority in the church. Many cite Paul's directive to apostles in 1 Timothy 2:11–12: 'I do not permit a woman to teach or to exercise authority over a man; rather, she is to remain quiet.'★ This passage, for them, effectively prohibits women from occupying any position of authority

---

★ The full passage is: 'Let a woman learn quietly with all submissiveness. I do not permit a woman to teach or to exercise authority over a man; rather, she is to remain quiet. For Adam was formed first, then Eve; and Adam was not deceived, but the woman was deceived and became a transgressor. Yet she will be saved through childbearing – if they continue in faith and love and holiness, with self-control.'

within the church. For them, the church should not be making women strong.

But Paul's directive was written 2,000 years ago, and there are many things in the Bible that have needed to be reinterpreted and developed with the passage of time. Indeed, Paul himself appointed many women in roles of authority in the early church, and women have proved themselves again and again through history to be some of the most formidable and doughty champions of the church, and strong women have often proved the bedrock of the faith in difficult times.

It's not just Christianity that had, in the past, attitudes against the idea of strong women, which should surely be put firmly behind us. Even Buddhism, one of the more egalitarian religions, insisted that 'A nun, even if she has been ordained for 100 years, must respect, greet and bow in reverence to the feet of a monk, even if he has just been ordained that day'.

It's pretty clear, though, that much of the religious effort to prevent women ever being strong came not from the founders of the religion but has been layered on through the centuries for various reasons that have very little to with theological constraints. Some of the most rampant attacks on women in positions of strength came from the Scottish Protestant reformer John Knox, who claimed that a curse would fall on any nation that was governed by a woman in his ferociously titled tract of 1558, *The First Blast of the Trumpet*

Against the Monstrous Regiment of Women. But he was writing when Britain fell under the rule of two Catholic Queen Marys – England's Mary Tudor and Scotland's Mary of Guise. So perhaps he felt rather threatened.

Fortunately, the world and religious attitudes have moved on. In spring 2014, the Church of England at last agreed to the idea of women bishops, and while the Arab Spring did little to improve attitudes to women in Egypt, in Tunisia it brought women into positions of authority for the first time as they took up seats in the newly elected parliament.

What makes a woman strong, then? I would say strength is physical and mental health in the broadest sense, not bogus toughness. And that comes from confidence – the confidence and sense of self to be entirely as you wish to be. To be brash and bold, or to be meek and gentle, to be wild, to be mild, to be funny, to be serious, to be graceful, to be awkward, to be quick, to be slow. Or all of these. To be the person you are. The strong woman is a stereotype as trapping in some ways as the fragile flower, but we should want all women to be strong – and for that strength they need, just like men, proper sustenance and nurturing, in everything from basic human needs to access to education or community support.

Why did Henry VII call his son Arthur?

(History, Oxford)

When Henry VII's first son was born on 20 September 1486, many people, at least in Henry's camp, must have breathed a sigh of relief. With Richard III's defeat and death at the Battle of Bosworth the previous year, the bloody struggles of the Wars of the Roses seemed to be at an end. For decades the country had been torn apart as the two arms of the Plantagenet dynasty, Lancaster and York, slugged it out. But Bosworth was surely the death knell of the Yorkist cause and the end of the Plantagenet dynasty. The hurt was still red raw and resentments deep, but there was a halt, at least, to the strife. And the birth of the prince to the still-young Henry seemed to secure the succession for at least a generation.

No doubt, though, a few eyebrows were raised when Henry chose to name the baby Arthur. After all, the royal family still had very strong French connections, and princes were more typically named Edward or Henry or Geoffrey. Arthur was an unusually British name. However, there could have been one very simple explanation. Arthur was actually the name on everyone's lips.

Just over a year previously, about the time of Bosworth, the pioneering printer William Caxton had made a bold step and published an entirely new book.

Sir Thomas Malory's *Le Morte d'Arthur* turned out to be the first big blockbuster in English, and by the time of the young prince's birth it was already creating quite a buzz. Stirring and romantic, it told the story of the legendary British king Arthur, and his Knights of the Round Table. Malory's genius was to blend the historicity of earlier Arthurian chronicles with the floridness of the French romance tradition to create a clear prose version that had the immediacy and pace of a novel. Printing ensured many people were able to read it within the first year of publication – and many more heard it read, and thrilled to the heroism and nobility of Arthur and Galahad, or felt their heartstrings plucked by the tragedy of Lancelot and Guinevere's doomed love.

So it wouldn't be surprising if the young king and queen might want to name their new baby after King Arthur, the new popular hero of the age, just as so many couples named their babies Harry after the celebrity of J.K. Rowling's boy wizard. It'd be a great start in life for the young prince to be linked to such a popular icon.

But there was probably more to it than that. Arthur wasn't just a fictional hero. In the story, and chronicles, he is presented as a genuine historical figure who lived around the 6th or 7th century. He was not English, but British, a Celt who brought order out of the chaos left by the departure of the Romans, and held out in the west against the tide of invading Anglo-Saxons. In the chronicles, he is the true, original king who heroically defended the country against the interlopers, and presided over a legendary glorious time.

This was a perfect connection for Henry and the Tudors. The Tudors emerged from Wales to seize the English crown, and their claim on the throne was much weaker than Richard's had been. So Henry got genealogists to trace the Tudor line back to Arthur, the true British king with his stronghold in Wales, and so put a stamp on their legitimacy as the true heirs of the British monarchy. It was certainly no accident that the little Prince Arthur was made Prince of Wales when he was just three. After all, Henry himself had ridden through London after Bosworth flying the red dragon banner of the ancient Welsh king Cadwaladr alongside the cross of St George – dragon and dragon-slayer in one.

It probably didn't really matter so much that many people might have been sceptical about the veracity of the Arthurian genealogy and the whole Welsh Arthur connection. By naming the young prince Arthur, Henry was making enough of a link to Britain's most glorified king, and making it less likely that his position would be challenged.

It was all about image-building. In fact, the Tudors became the first monarchical dynasty who really went to town with branding for bringing people on side. Not just Henry VII, but Henry VIII and Elizabeth embarked on what today might be called a massive PR campaign, filled with conspicuous displays of pageantry and magnificence, to enhance their glory and splendour, and so consolidate their power.

Arthur's birth was presented as the beginning of a new golden age, a Virgilian age, when British culture would flower as before only in King Arthur's legendary Camelot. The image was not warlike but cultural and luxurious, as if the Tudors had enabled the kingdom to turn a corner from the martial times of yore. Henry drew artists from Europe such as Pietro Torrigiano and encouraged English craftsmen to begin a remarkable English Renaissance in which the new Prince Arthur would emerge as the hero. Gradually, the Tudors began to create an aura of glamour that made England and the English court admired and envied across Europe.

Arthur, though, would not live to see the coming of the new Tudor Camelot. He died, of what might have been TB, in 1602, aged just sixteen, at Ludlow on the borders of Wales, leaving his younger brother Henry to become king as Henry VIII and eclipse maybe even the legendary Arthur with the sheer size of his personality – a king at once both splendid and appalling. Arthur, meanwhile, is largely forgotten. Even the re-enactment of his funeral with a requiem mass at Worcester Cathedral on the occasion of the quincentenary of his death in 2002 raised barely a ripple of interest.

How would you compare Henry VIII and Stalin? *(History, Cambridge)*

Both King Henry VIII and Stalin tower over the history of their countries like giants, but physically there was no comparison. Henry was a huge man, especially for Tudor times. He was over 1.9m (6ft 3in) tall, and dwarfed his courtiers. And later in life he was massive widthways too, weighing not far short of 140kg (22 stone) and measuring over 130cm (50in) around the waist. Stalin, on the other hand, was elevationally challenged, maybe less than 1.6m (5ft 3in) tall, and wore platform shoes or stood on a box to make up for his lack of stature.

Until he was 40 or more, Henry was also extremely athletic, renowned for his skill at wrestling and archery, while Stalin had a short and permanently stiff left arm. So if it came to hand-to-hand combat between Big Hal and Little Joe, your money would have to be on the Brit. Mind you, Stalin had an army of more than 10 million to back him up, not to mention tanks and acroplanes; Henry's army was barely a thousandth the size and armed just with pikes, bows and arquebusses.

The serious intent of a comparison, though, is between their regimes, to see if it helps us understand either a little more. The comparison is much more illuminating about Henry than Stalin, though. Henry has been called the Tudor Stalin – but one can't imagine Stalin being called the Russian Henry.

The idea of Henry as the Tudor Stalin originated with landscape historian W.G. Hoskins. Hoskins disagreed with the popular portrayal of Merrie England with its colourful costumes and bawdy songs, and Henry VIII as a roguish buffoon as in the famous 1933 film *The Private Life of Henry VIII*, which starred comedian Charles Laughton as the king. He wanted to make the point that life in England under Henry was as frightening and nasty as Stalin's Russia.

There are indeed similarities. Both in Stalin's Russia and in Henry's England, a revolution was being forced through brutally. Stalin, of course, was driving through communism, and Henry the break from the Catholic church. Both leaders could argue, and did, that this was rough medicine which would rid the people of a vile and corrupt regime – Stalin the tsars and aristocrats, Henry the power of the Pope and the worst abuses of the monasteries. The country needed to be purged of the sickness in order to create a better, healthier world.

Neither Stalin's regime nor Henry tolerated any objection to their activities or even their opinions. Any hint of opposition was silenced with extraordinary cruelty. Both had ruthless right-hand men to do their dirty work and set up networks of spies and informers to catch any backsliders or threats. For Stalin, it was Beria and the NKVD who terrorised the country. For Henry, it was Thomas Cromwell and the Star Chamber. Little evidence was needed to fall foul of Cromwell or Beria.

A hint here, a misplaced word there was enough to get you condemned, and of course those who wouldn't talk could always have their tongues loosened by torture. There was a constant atmosphere of fear and distrust, since you could never be sure who would betray you and speak against you. There were trials and hearings in both Stalin's Russia and Henry's England, but the chances of a fair hearing were slim.

The form of retribution, though, was very, very different. There were no gulags in Henry's England, or years of hard labour. Nor were there were many secret assassinations, or being whisked away in the dead of night. Instead, victims of Henry's regime were executed, very publicly and horrifically. Each execution was meant to be a frightening example to would-be traitors, the more gruesome the better. People were hung, drawn and quartered, or even boiled alive. When Henry executed his wife Anne, he considered it merciful to have her merely beheaded with a sword.

No one can be sure of the numbers executed under Henry. The chronicler Raphael Holinshed insisted in the 1570s that it was 72,000, with more than a thousand executions a week in the 1530s. But there is little evidence either way. Most historians suspect the numbers were far fewer. England only had a population of 3 million at the time, so the threat of being caught up in the maelstrom was very real.

Yet the scale of the purges in Stalin's Russia is

immeasurably different. The numbers involved are of course appallingly huge. Many millions died in Stalin's Russia and millions more spent horrific years in the gulags. But even that doesn't touch the vast numbers of lives blighted, the lives lived in fear, the lives robbed of moments of happiness.

Henry's regime was brutal and severe, but its impact on ordinary people was, on the whole, limited. It was only those unlucky enough to come into the sphere of court influence or, like Robert Aske's Pilgrimage of Grace, challenge Henry in outright rebellion who felt its full nastiness. For most people – the ordinary peasants and yeoman farmers, the merchants and craftsmen, the minor gentry and landowners – life went on much as before with its normal share of hardships, but no more. Indeed, for many it was a time of considerable prosperity. And for all those who were devastated by the destruction of the monasteries, there were probably many more who were quite happy to see them go, since the grievances against them were genuine.

England was a rural country, a country of small towns and villages, in which the big issues of the day had little direct impact. The full effect of Stalin's regime was a constant reality in every city across the Soviet Union, changing lives dramatically – and of course it reached far across rural Russia too as his forced agricultural plans brought famine on an unimaginable scale. Really, there is not even the remotest comparison between the mass fear, misery and suffering, the sense of widespread desperation affecting vast numbers of people in Stalin's Russia and the isolated cruelty and troubles of Henry's England.

Stalin's rule brought genocide on an appalling scale, and forced migration of millions of people. His regime imposed systematic and totalitarian control on a vast scale. Henry's attacks were localised and even personal and the comparisons with Stalin's Russia are glib rather than genuinely illuminating. For all the brutality and danger of Henry's rule, there is a sense of morality afoot. Thomas More died a martyr of his conscience, but he was operating in a moral climate where he could have a conscience, and could make the choice to die a martyr. In Stalin's Russia, the complete breakdown in values seems to have created a moral vacuum in which only survival mattered.

Personally, too, Henry and Stalin were vastly different people. Stalin was brought up in a fairly poor family in Georgia very far from the centres of power in St Petersburg. He rose to the top through dramatically changing circumstances and his own force of will. He was leader of Russia because he and those he worked with made it happen. Henry was a royal prince who became king because his older brother Arthur died. He was king by the will of God. His life was always one of luxury and pleasure. He had the freedom to be charming and fun-loving, the freedom to dance and listen to music, and compose the beautiful song 'Greensleeves', as well as marry six women and flirt with and make love to many more. Power was as easy and natural to Henry as the rain. There could not be a greater contrast to the dour life of Stalin who had to claw his way to the top, and had to fight every minute of the day and night to reinforce his position, and had little time for luxuries and pastimes.

The historian Geoffrey Elton painted Henry out of the centre of his reign. Elton saw Henry as far too weak a ruler to be a monster – too vain and inconstant, too caught up in the pleasures of the table and the bed. The real power was in the hands of ambitious courtiers and cardinals – men like Thomas Cromwell. That view has had to be revised recently, as papers reveal how active a hand Henry had in imposing sanctions and choosing methods of executions.

It can be instructive to reinterpret historical events in the light of later ones we know more about. We can gain a new perspective on Henry's regime by stripping away the pageant, pomp and religion and seeing it in terms of 20th-century realpolitik and power-mongering. But there's a danger of us getting carried away by the cleverness of our own comparisons, and seeing connections that are perhaps only superficial.

Anyway, whatever the dangers of Henry's regime, I find the idea of his time far more appealing than Stalin's. Maybe it's the romance from historical fiction.

Maybe it's the costumes. Maybe it's the sense that beautiful things could be created in Henry's regime, so different from the drab brutalism of Stalin's industrialisation. But maybe when I was having my genitals severed and my bowels ripped out, I'd long for the peace of the gulag …

Why do you think Charlotte Brontë detested Jane Austen? *(English, Cambridge)*

Poor Charlotte Brontë. She expressed her views about Jane Austen in private letters to the writer-philosopher George Henry Lewes in response to a rather patronising review Lewes wrote of *Jane Eyre* in the influential *Westminster Review* in 1847. Brontë, he wrote, might benefit from writing a little less melodramatically – and he urged her to follow the example of Jane Austen, who in his mind, was 'the greatest artist who has ever written', and that 'to read one of her books is like an actual experience of life'. *Jane Eyre* was Brontë's first novel, and being held up against this exemplar of novelistic art in such a way must have hurt like hell. Stung, Brontë wrote to Lewes to defend herself in what she no doubt thought were measured terms – and what she wrote has had Austen fans heaping criticism on her ever since.

'I had not seen *Pride and Prejudice* till I read that sentence of yours,' Brontë wrote, 'and then I got the book and studied it. And what did I find? An accurate daguerrotyped portrait of a common-place face; a carefully-fenced, highly cultivated garden with neat borders and delicate flowers – but no glance of a bright vivid physiognomy – no open country – no fresh air – no blue hill – no bonny beck. I should hardly like to live with her ladies and gentlemen in their elegant but confined houses.'

In other words, Charlotte Brontë thought Jane Austen was all very nice and clever and shrewd, but that was it. Charlotte was brought up on the wild, windswept Yorkshire moors, full of dark skies and foul winters when everyone was confined indoors. Her entertainment was not balls, visits to friends nearby, conversation and cards, but private reading and flights of imagination, and long, long, weatherbeaten walks. Jane Austen was brought up far to the south, in the mild climes of Hampshire, where society was lively but light and even a brief shower while out strolling would cause consternation. Two more contrasting lives could not be imagined – and it is hardly surprising that Charlotte should react badly when told she should be like someone whose life she could barely imagine, let alone understand.

To Charlotte, it must have seemed that when Lewes criticised her melodrama, he was really saying she was unsophisticated and parochial next to the urbane restraint and control of Miss Austen. No wonder she came out fighting. Far away in the north, she was cut off from the sophisticated intellectuals of London, and this championing of Austen would no doubt seem to be shutting her out of the elite circle.

On the surface, their personalities and approach to writing could not be more different. So it is hardly surprising Charlotte had little time for Jane. Today, they are bracketed together as the pinnacles of romantic costume drama, the lady authors whose novels provide the basis for Sunday evening nostalgia fests on TV. But, initially at least it seems, they are hugely contrasting writers.

Charlotte seems the very embodiment of the tortured romantic image of the writer, scribbling her dark tales of passion high up on the lonely moors. The Romantic writers that she and her siblings grew up reading – Byron, Shelley, Wordsworth – saw themselves as figures apart, solitary and perhaps misunderstood, but looked to nature and a rich inner life for inspiration. Keen to shed the pettiness and squalor of city life, Romantic poets had ventured out alone to seek an elemental truth and purity in nature in the remotest countryside. Charlotte and her sisters had no need to – they were already there. For the Romantics she and her sister adored, the poet is a god on Earth, their imagination the power to create and open minds to better worlds beyond the pain of this. And like nature, love for Romantics was transcendent, overwhelming, everlasting – never common, often painful, frequently tragic and always difficult, whether unreturned or star-crossed by circumstance.

By contrast, Jane Austen is, at least superficially, Augustan, classical in her restraint, urbane, witty, light. Hers is a quiet, civilised world where Lydia Bennett's elopement with the dangerous Wickham in *Pride and Prejudice* is not a grand passion but a silly adolescent embarrassment. Kisses are rare and gentle and never overwhelming. Bad weather is an inconvenience, not an inspiration. Heroines suffer, but they do not experience agonising torment.

No wonder then that Charlotte found Jane Austen insipid, writing about Austen after reading *Emma*, 'the Passions are perfectly unknown to her; she rejects even a speaking acquaintance with that stormy Sisterhood; even to the Feelings she vouchsafes no more than an occasional graceful but distant recognition; too frequent converse with them would ruffle the smooth elegance of her progress.' Ouch.

But of course Charlotte did have an axe to grind with the thoughtless George Lewes, who kept on berating her with Miss Austen, and reviewed her second book *Shirley* as tepidly as he had *Jane Eyre*, whilst carelessly letting slip to his circle the secret that its author Currer Bell was in fact Charlotte. So it's unlikely she could ever have read Jane Austen without prejudice.

If she had, she might have found more to identify with. For a start, her own novels are not quite the grand, granite-hewn romantic melodrama of her sister Emily's *Wuthering Heights* with its Byronic anti-hero Heathcliff – a book Charlotte herself criticised as immature and rough in much the same way Lewes criticised hers in comparison to Jane Austen's. And Lucy Snowe in Charlotte's *Villette*, quiet and determined, does not seem so many worlds away from an Austen heroine such as Fanny Price in *Mansfield Park*. And interestingly, in both *Mansfield Park* and *Jane Eyre*, the heroine is a governess, a neglected and underappreciated outsider, treated cruelly as a child.

Both writers were, in their own way, champions of women, writers who gave women characters intelligent minds and hearts of their own, who wrote about women who wanted to make their own choices in love and life. A review of the film *Pride and Prejudice* with Keira Knightley suggested that the film had 'Brontëfied' Austen, implying that the urbane restraint of Jane Austen had been given a modern makeover, with a more melodramatic, sexier spin. Austen might have felt this was manufactured passion, and distrusted it as macho, imposing on women just as Wickham once imposed on Elizabeth Bennett – and Charlotte, who has Jane Eyre run away when Rochester gets too full-on, might have agreed. Jane can only return to Rochester when he is maimed and more restrained. Both Jane Austen and Charlotte Brontë refuse to allow their heroines to settle with domineering men; such men must first be tamed. So, perhaps, had they ever met, Charlotte might have found she had more in common with Jane than she would ever admit. As Charlotte wrote in *The Professor*, 'You know full well as I do the value of sisters' affections: There is nothing like it in this world.'

If you are in a boat in a lake and throw a stone out of the boat, what happens to the level of the water? *(Medicine, Cambridge)*

Of course, one can imagine all kinds of fanciful scenarios. Why might you be throwing the stone from the boat? Could you be in a foul mood because you just received a text from your lover saying it's over? Or could the old boat be shipping water fast and you're desperately trying to stop it sinking? How big is the stone? Is it so big that when you chuck it in, the splash and ripple send water surging over the lake banks? Or do you actually throw the stone far enough to land on the shore?

But maybe we should just treat this as a simple physics problem. If so, it's all to do with Archimedes' Principle. The discovery of this principle is one of the great, apocryphal stories of science. Archimedes lived in Syracuse in the 3rd century BC, and it seems he was the very prototype of the absent-minded scientist, so absorbed in high thoughts that he forgot about everyday needs. According to Plutarch, 'He was so bewitched by thought that he always forgot to eat and ignored his appearance. When things became too bad his friends would forcibly insist that he had a bath, and make sure that afterwards he anointed himself with sweet smelling oils. Yet even then he would remain lost to the world, drawing geometric figures.'

And it was in one of those bath-time moments that Archimedes came upon his principle, as it were. According to Vitruvius, who was telling the story some two centuries later (so might have got it wrong), the Syracusan King Hieron asked a goldsmith to fashion a wreath from a chunk of gold. When the goldsmith returned with the wreath, it looked great, but Hieron suspected the crafty goldsmith had pocketed some of the gold and mixed in some cheaper metal instead. Yet the wreath weighed exactly the same as the original chunk of gold. How then could the fraud be proved? Hieron asked Archimedes, and Archimedes mulled it over. Then one day, while mulling away in his bath, he saw how the water level rose as he sunk deeper into the bath.

Not one to bother with towels or clothes or other niceties, Archimedes leaped straight from his bath and ran naked through the streets to the king, shouting at the top of his voice, *Eureka! Eureka!* ('I've got it! I've got it!'). For sheer theatricality, that completely trounces the best Premier League goal celebrations or Usain Bolt's lightning moments.

This was the idea that Archimedes got, as Vitruvius tells it. First he immersed in water a piece of gold that weighed the same as the wreath. Then he immersed the wreath itself and discovered that the water level rose further. This meant the wreath must have a greater volume than the gold, even if it was the same weight.

So it could not be pure gold. The unfortunate gold-smith was executed.

One thousand eight hundred years later, Galileo questioned this story. Ingenious though it is, it didn't seem nearly reliable enough for someone as meticulously scientific and precise as Archimedes. Nonetheless, whether completely true or not, Archimedes did go on to make groundbreaking – or rather water-breaking – discoveries about buoyancy and why things float.

Archimedes' great insight was that an object weighs less in water than in air. When an object is immersed in water, its weight pulls it down. But the water, as Archimedes realised, pushes back up with a force equal to the weight of water the object pushes out of the way. The pressure of the water surrounding anything immersed in water creates an upthrust. So a boat sinks until its weight is exactly equal to the upthrust of the water, at which point it floats. Objects that weigh less than the water displaced will float; those that weigh more will sink. Archimedes showed this is a precise and easily calculated mathematical relationship.

It's all about the relationship between the weight of the immersed object and the volume of water displaced. A steel-hulled ship floats, even though steel itself is too dense to float, because the hull is hollow and so allows the ship to displace so much water that it creates enough upthrust to float the weight of steel.

Our conundrum with the stone follows on from

this. When it's in the boat, the stone adds to the boat's weight, and so the boat displaces an amount of water that weighs the same as the boat including the stone. In other words, when it's in the boat, the stone displaces a volume of water that weighs exactly the same.

When you throw it overboard, however, something different happens. We're going to assume it's not a pumice stone and light enough to float. If it's a normal, dense stone, it will sink to the bottom of the lake, frightening a few fish on the way down, no doubt. When it's totally immersed, it will no longer displace a volume of water the same as its weight; it will only displace a volume of water the same as its own volume. Since the stone is denser than water, it means the volume of water displaced is less. That means the level of the lake should drop very slightly – because the total volume of water displaced by the boat with the stone on the bottom of the lake is marginally less than the total volume of water displaced by the boat when it's carrying the stone. But if you fell overboard while chucking the stone in, things just got a whole lot more complicated ...

Are Fairtrade bananas really fair?

(Geography, Oxford)

People in the developed world are often shocked and appalled when they hear about the extent of poverty in the undeveloped countries of the world. They look at their own relatively comfortable lives and feel they must be able to do something to help. Charity is good for the short term, but most people simply want the world to be a fairer place, for people to get just rewards for their labour and to be able to work and get a decent income. And it's this basic idea of fairness that is behind the Fairtrade movement.

Back in the 13th century, Thomas Aquinas talked about the idea of a 'just price'. A dealer, he asserted, may charge a 'just' price that includes a decent profit, but excessive profiteering is sinful. But he proposed that a just price is simply the price the buyer freely agrees to pay. Modern market economists, on the other hand, insist that there is no moral dimension to pricing at all – it is simply an automatic response to the balance between supply and demand. Any pricing that is not simply an automatic reflection of supply and demand interferes with the clear workings of the free market. Yet most of us have a very definite view of what is a 'fair' price and what is not. We may not use the term 'just', but we are still sensitive to the notion of being 'ripped off'. Similarly, many of us know that the fairness should go both ways – and that producers should not be ripped off either. In recent years, economists have been forced to readjust their ideas to acknowledge that ethical considerations do play a part.

The Fairtrade movement grew out of the awareness that one reason for hardship in the underdeveloped world was that producers were being ripped off. Consumers knew they were paying high prices for food products such as coffee and bananas in the shops, but were also learning that very little of that seemed to be going to the poor farmers who actually grew it.

A decade ago, in a report aptly entitled *Mugged*, Oxfam traced the prices paid for a kilo of coffee grown in Uganda in 2002. The farmer was paid fourteen US cents. The local miller took an extra five cents, while transport and other costs meant that the exporter bought it for 26 cents. The exporter graded and packaged it and sold it on for 45 cents. By the time it reached the big multinational who would roast the coffee and turn it into instant coffee granules, the price was $1.64. But that same kilo of coffee would sell in shops in instant form at an astonishing $26.40 – that is, nearly 200 times more than the farmer got for it. The idea of the Fairtrade movement was to deploy consumer choice to ensure that a much higher proportion of that final price went directly to the producer, as surveys of consumers showed a high proportion were willing to pay at least a small premium to ensure it happened.

It wasn't just about price, though. In many banana-producing countries, smallholders are squeezed out by the big plantations, or find themselves at the mercy of tough middlemen. Wages on the plantations in countries like Ecuador and Costa Rica are pushed to rock bottom, and there are suggestions that young children are employed to work long hours on banana plantations. Worse still, pesticides and fungicides are in widespread use, both to ensure the 'perfect' bananas supermarkets demand and to combat the diseases and pests that become increasingly a problem as production intensifies. Labourers suffer depression and respiratory problems due to exposure to these chemicals. Moreover, there is a real worry that bananas could be entirely wiped out by disease.

The Fairtrade movement started off very small scale, with a handful of producers producing coffee and similar products for sale directly through charities such as Oxfam. The involvement of a trusted charity with known links direct to the producers seemed to be enough for consumers to trust that producers were being paid a better, fairer pricer. But the movement really took off when the idea of certification was introduced. Certification meant that consumers could buy Fairtrade products in mainstream shops such as supermarkets and still have a degree of confidence that the same principles were in operation. It started with Fairtrade coffee, which has now swelled to more than a fifth of all coffee sales. But in the UK in particular, it is Fairtrade bananas which have really boomed. Supermarket chains such as Sainsbury's and Waitrose sell only Fairtrade bananas, and nearly two thirds of UK consumers buy at least some Fairtrade bananas each year.

With trading on this scale, it is really important to know whether the idea is really delivering – whether Fairtrade bananas are really fair for both producers and consumers. Various studies have been done, such as that by Sally Smith of the Institute of Development Studies at the University of Sussex, and that by Kimberly Elliott of the Centre for Global Development. What these studies show is that it is surprisingly hard to unravel just how well the system does work.

One issue, for instance, is price variation. One of the ideas behind Fairtrade was to guarantee a fixed price upfront to save the producer being battered by fluctuations in the market price. That was a great help when the world price for, say, bananas was low, or dropping. But now, when banana prices are higher, it does not seem so beneficial, since producers might get a higher price on the open market, yet are locked into a deal through the Fairtrade route.

Another issue is that Fairtrade certification demands certain things of producers, such as a ban on forced and child labour and on GM crops. However right such restrictions seem to consumers, producers may feel them an unfair imposition that is insensitive to local needs.

Producers have to pay a high price to ensure Fairtrade certification, which might seem unfair on those unable to afford the premium. But it helps guarantee commitment on both sides. The fact that increasing numbers of producers are willing to pay for certification suggests that they at least think it is worthwhile. But the studies suggest the benefits to producers are not quite what the consumer of Fairtrade bananas might expect. Fairtrade doesn't always directly raise income and improve working conditions, for instance. Instead, it works by providing producers with better access and information about markets. It also gives many workers better social status and a sense of security by turning casual jobs into formal contracted employment. The effect on these permanent workers seems to be marked and beneficial. However, migrant workers and those less able to take up fixed jobs seem to suffer in comparison.

Overall, though, the impression is that Fairtrade bananas have been genuinely beneficial. According to Sally Smith, 'Positive impacts have occurred [from Fairtrade of bananas] at all levels from individuals to households, to local communities and national economies, [helping small producers especially to] stabilise their income, improve their production, gain direct access to markets and participate more actively in organisations and networks.'

Perhaps the most dramatic side of it all has been the power of consumer choice to change attitudes. Supermarkets have stocked and promoted Fairtrade products because it is good for their image to do so, and increasingly they are seeing 'ethical' and 'sustainable' sourcing as valuable marketing tools. The success of Fairtrade bananas in the UK marketplace in particular – matched by Fairtrade coffee in countries like Switzerland – shows just what the ordinary buyer can do to help make the world a fairer place. The reaction of some clothing companies to the tragedy of the factory collapse in Rana Plaza in Bangladesh in 2013 shows just how sensitive Western retailers have needed to become to any links with exploitation of workers in the underdeveloped world. The scale of Fairtrade is still very small, but it's a start.

How does geography relate to *A Midsummer Night's Dream*?

(Geography, Oxford)

Of course, the very title of this, Shakespeare's most fantastical and otherworldly play, is geographic. The play is not set on just any night, but *Midsummer Night*. Midsummer Night had mystical significance, dating back to ancient times. It reveals that Shakespeare's England, superficially Christian, had pagan roots that run far, far deeper, and this whole play is a wonderful celebration of this night when magic is in the air, and faeries and sprites are abroad.

Midsummer Night is the summer solstice, and the very special alignment of the sun at this point is celebrated and noted in countless stone circles and ancient monuments in Britain and beyond. Stonehenge is a monument entirely arranged, most experts believe, to honour the solstice, which is why even today thousands of people go there at dawn on Midsummer's Day to witness the sun striking through the gap in the ancient stones.

Geographically, of course, the summer solstice is the longest day of the year, the day when the sun rises earlier, climbs higher at noon and sets later than on any other day of the year. But what those people at Stonehenge are noting is its most northerly sunrise of the year, the furthest extent of its annual journey.

So the summer solstice is the turning point of the year, the *sol stice* – Latin for 'sun stand'. Throughout the first half of the year in the northern hemisphere, the sun rises and sets further and further north each day. Then on Midsummer's Day, its northward journey seems to come momentarily to a standstill before reversing and moving south again day by day until the winter solstice, the summer solstice's dark opposite, the shortest day of the year, six months later.

Of course, it's not the sun moving at all, but the Earth, whirling past on its epic annual elliptical journey. Because it's tilted over, the angle at which we see the sun from anywhere on Earth constantly shifts. And so it seems as if the path the sun traces through the sky each day shifts, whereas it is just the Earth moving on its orbit and revealing the sun at a slightly different angle.

You can tell you are facing the sun directly, and that its rays are striking perpendicularly when you can see it at its highest point in the sky, its zenith, directly overhead at noon. As the Earth swings around the sun, so the line around the Earth at which this happens travels north and south across the equator. The summer solstice in the northern hemisphere is when it reaches the Tropic of Cancer, its furthest point north. The summer solstice in the southern hemisphere is when it reaches the Tropic of Capricorn six months later, the time of the winter solstice in the north.

Of course, these shifts of the sun are not just

astronomical features. They bring us the seasons. Throughout the year until the summer solstice, the sun climbs higher, making the days longer and the weather generally warmer, and moving us from winter through spring and into summer. But after the solstice, the sun begins to drop again and the days get shorter and cooler into autumn and then winter. It's the sense of this life's cycle reaching its climax that made Midsummer's Night so special and magical, and the feeling that anything might happen.

Shakespeare, of course, plays loose with his geography. That's always the case. Although he sets his plays in Verona and Venice, Ephesus and Elsinore, one never really gets much sense of these places as they really were, and that's hardly surprising, since there is no evidence that Shakespeare travelled much outside England, if at all. These places are just exotic settings to create a sense of distance and wonder. But in *A Midsummer Night's Dream*, he throws all pretence at geographical accuracy to the winds.

The play starts in Athens, and the magical wood is supposedly set just beyond the city. But Athens never seems like that sun-baked city on the Aegean with its temple ruins. And the magic wood where the lovers spend the night is as far from Athens as magic could transport you. It is a very English wood, like the Forest of Arden Shakespeare knew so well. And it is described with a vivacity and love for its nature that only someone who has walked those woods since childhood and was intimate with its changing moods could achieve. The wildflowers Oberon tells of are those of an English wood, described by someone who had observed their habits closely:

> I know a bank where the wild thyme blows,
> Where oxlips and the nodding violet grows,
> Quite over-canopied with luscious woodbine,
> With sweet musk-roses and with eglantine:

Shakespeare was intimately acquainted with English weather, too, as you might expect from someone who grew up in the country and whose plays were performed in the open air. But his weather observation is accurate.

Titania, when she describes the chaos in the weather caused by her upset with Oberon, describes it in terms that anyone who knew the English weather would recognise.* She talks about winds sucking fogs from the sea, for instance. Maybe she's talking of a haar or sea fret, one of those mists that rolls in from the sea on

---

* For example:

'Therefore the winds, piping to us in vain,
As in revenge, have suck'd up from the sea
Contagious fogs; which falling in the land
Have every pelting river made so proud
That they have overborne their continents'.　　(Act II, Scene 1)

summer days on the east coast of England. They form
when a parcel of warm air blows over the cool North
Sea, making moisture in the lower layers condense to
form a mist; and the warmth of the land compared to
the sea draws this haze inland, just as Titania describes.
It's these frets and haars that can make summers here
as miserable as she laments.

Shakespeare's play is set in a topsy-turvy, magical world, but it is a world that has its roots in a deep
acquaintance with the world of nature, an English landscape in which the seasons turn, weather blows harsh
and mild, and the flowers, in their own ecosystem, have
each their place. It's this that makes Shakespeare's play
so much more resonant and memorable than any mere
fantasy.

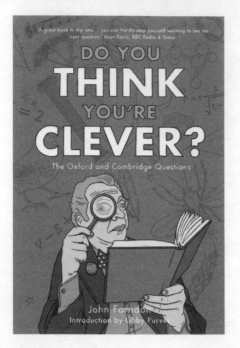